CU00596964

Acknowledgements

I am, as ever, immensely grateful to Peter and Jackie Fennymore help in preparing this book and to Rupert Fennymore for his wo.......... ....
I should like also to thank Peter Brown of Trinity College, Oxford for his unfailing readiness to face with his great learning and common sense, questions with which I have pelted him at all hours of day and night. Once again I am extremely grateful to Nicholas Oulton for the constant courtesy, patience and good sense with which he has ensured, I hope, the usefulness of this volume. Finally, special thanks are due to Bill Inge of Ashfold School and Michael Webb of Northbourne Park School who read the proofs of this book with meticulous care and attention to detail. I need hardly add that all errors are mine and mine alone.

Preface

I must admit that the more involved I have become in the subject-matter of this book, the more I have found myself having to walk a tight-rope between saying too much and saying too little. I regard it as a duty never to say anything which is positively untrue, but I feel justified in, for example, leaving the finest points of the pronunciation of some parts of *hic* for a later volume. At least, on the positive side, I hope that, with the increased syllabus-content at my disposal, I have managed to improve my stories a little. I have included just a very few sections (such as the one on *praenomina*) which are not strictly required by the syllabus - these can easily be skipped. I have also included a list of proper nouns and adjectives, many (but not all) of which are also given in the vocabularies and notes that accompany the passages in which they occur.

I am immensely grateful for the kind words about Latin Prep 1 which have reached my ears and I only hope that this volume, too, will give pleasure to more and more students of the Latin language, all of whom have my very best wishes.

TLZ, April 2004

Contents

Chapter 1

salvē, salvē: greetings!

I knew we'd meet again, and I hope you're as glad about it as I am. I have so many treats for you that I hardly know where to start. However, remember the 3rd conjugation of verbs, with all those nasty tricks up its sleeve? Well, the 3rd declension of nouns is rather like it. (Hurray! I'm sure you welcome the challenge.) So, let's deal with it now while you're fresh and ready for the fray.

The 3rd declension: rēx

		rēx, rēgis, m. = 'king'	
		Singular	**Plural**
	Nominative	*rēx*	*rēgēs*
	Vocative	*rēx*	*rēgēs*
	Accusative	*rēgem*	*rēgēs*
	Genitive	*rēgis*	*rēgum*
	Dative	*rēgī*	*rēgibus*
	Ablative	*rēge*	*rēgibus*

We shall use the word 'stem' for the form on to which the different case endings are added. We can see immediately that the stem of *rēx* is not as easily identifiable as was the stem of *puella,* namely *puell-,* or that of *dominus,* namely *domin-.* Here we have to dig *rēg-* out of *rēx,* (the *'x'* here represents *'gs'*). Indeed, every time we learn a 3rd declension noun, we must give extra-special attention to learning its genitive singular, which, once we have chopped off the '*-is*' ending, will always reveal its stem.

We should point out that the choice of *rēx* as our model noun is far from tactful. The Romans had an abiding hatred of kings, having had an unpleasant experience of them in their early history, and poor old Julius Caesar was murdered precisely because his enemies thought that he was trying to make himself a king.

Exercise 1.1

Set out the following nouns in full, as *rēx* is set out on the previous page. Remember to identify the stem of each noun before trying to add the endings. e.g. *lūx, lūcis*, f.: stem = *lūc-*

1. *lūx, lūcis*, f. = light
2. *vōx, vōcis*, f. = voice
3. *dux, ducis*, c. = leader, general, captain
4. *comes, comitis*, c. = companion
5. *coniūnx, coniugis*, c. = wife/husband
6. *clāmor, clāmōris*, m. = shout

N.B.
(i)   The '*i*' of *coniūnx* is consonantal, i.e. pronounced like 'y' in 'yes'.
(ii) The common nouns were regularly treated as masculine, unless the sense required them to be feminine. We shall do the same in this book, though we regret that the Romans were not very good at political correctness.

Exercise 1.2

Translate into Latin:

1. Of a king
2. Of the leaders
3. A companion (acc.)
4. With the wife
5. With a husband
6. To the kings (dat.)
7. In the light
8. Into the light
9. Oh, leaders!
10. Of the companions
11. Of the wives
12. With the leaders
13. The voice (acc.)
14. Of the old man
15. Oh, companions!
16. Oh, companion!
17. Towards the light
18. Out of the light
19. Oh, king!
20. Oh, kings!

And here are some more 3rd declension nouns that go like *rēx:*

mīles, mīlitis, c. = soldier
homō, hominis, c. = human being, man/woman
senex, senis, m. = old man
iuvenis, iuvenis, c. = young person (m. = a youth, young man)
virtūs, virtūtis, f. = courage, manly virtue
mulier, mulieris, f. = woman
uxor, uxōris, f. = wife

Exercise 1.3

Fill in the gaps in the following vocabulary list:

1. *uxor, uxōris*, f. = ...
2. *virtūs, ...,* f. = courage, manly virtue
3. *..., hominis*, c. = human being, man/woman
4. *comes, comitis, ...* = companion
5. *clāmor, clāmōris, ...* = shout
6. *mīles, ...,* c. = soldier
7. *..., senis*, m. = old man
8. *lūx, lūcis, ...* = light

Exercise 1.4

Translate into Latin:

1. Of the soldier
2. Of the man
3. Of the old men
4. The women (nom.)
5. The wives (acc.)
6. To the young man (dat.)
7. To the young men (dat.)
8. Oh! soldiers
9. By courage
10. With the wives

11. Of the soldiers
12. Of the men
13. Of the old man
14. The woman (acc.)
15. The wife (nom.)
16. To the youth (using *ad* + acc.)
17. To the youths (using *ad* + acc.)
18. Oh! soldier
19. Oh! old men
20. Oh! old man

Exercise 1.5

Translate into English:

1. *dux mīlitēs in proelium dūxit.*
2. *rēgēs saepe senēs sunt.*
3. *Laeliae coniūnx iuvenis erat.*
4. *in templō lūx nōn est.*
5. *comitēsne rēgis estis?*
6. *clāmōrem audīvī.*
7. *hominēs in viā stant.*
8. *bonī ducēs virtūtem habent.*
9. *virtūtem iuvenum laudāmus.*
10. *senex uxōrem nōn habet.*

Exercise 1.6

Translate into Latin:

1. Quintus, the poet, praises the king.
2. The young men gave help to the old man.
3. Where is the woman's husband?
4. The sailors were fighting with the soldiers.
5. The wife loved (her) dear husband.
6. The young men want to be soldiers.
7. There is a light in the sky.
8. The girls were the woman's companions.
9. The king praised the soldier's courage.
10. We did not hear the voice of the leader.

Family nouns

Here are four more nouns, giving us the family circle. They all go exactly like *rēx*, which, as we learn later, is slightly naughty of them.

pater, patris, m. = father
māter, mātris, f. = mother
frāter, frātris, m. = brother
soror, sorōris, f. = sister

Exercise 1.7

Read the following passage carefully, and answer the questions on it.

Wolf! Wolf! The shepherd's son is left at home alone

1   *pāstor erat, quī multās ovēs habuit; etiam fīlium habuit.*
    ōlim, ubi fīlius iam iuvenis fuit, pater discessit; et fīliō
    dīxit: 'ego nunc discēdō, et tū ovēs cūrāre dēbēs.'
    pāstōris fīlius stultus et timidus erat; lupōs magnopere
5   *timēbat. prope nostrum pāstōrem multī pāstōrēs*
    habitābant; et ubi lupī in stabulum venīre et ovēs
    cōnsūmere cupiēbant, dominus stabulī magnā vōce 'lupī
    adsunt!' clāmābat, 'lupī!' deinde multī pāstōrēs cum
    hastīs in stabulum festīnābant; et lupī perterritī
10 *fugiēbant.*

Remember the *pāstor,* Faustulus, who took the twins Romulus and Remus home to his wife? And the she-wolf (*lupa*) who had suckled them?

pāstor, pāstōris, m. = shepherd
quī = who
ovis, ovis, f. = sheep
nunc = now
cūrō, cūrāre, cūrāvī, cūrātum =
  I take care of
dēbeō, dēbēre, dēbuī, dēbitum
  (+ infin.) = I ought to, must
stultus, -a, -um = silly
timidus, -a, -um = timid
lupus, lupī, m. = wolf
stabulum, -ī, n. = stable
fugiō, fugere, fūgī, fugitum =
  I flee

1.   Answer the following questions fully:

   (a) In line 1, what did the shepherd possess?
   (b) In line 2, was his son still a boy at the time of this story?
   (c) In line 3, what does the shepherd tell his son he must do in his father's absence?
   (d) In lines 4-5, does the shepherd's son seem a suitable person to be left alone?
   (e) In lines 5-6, did our shepherd live far from other human beings?
   (f) In lines 6-7, why did wolves want to come into the stable?
   (g) In line 7, suggest a neat translation for *magnā vōce.*
   (h) In lines 8-9, what frightened the wolves?

2.   Translate the passage sheepishly.

3. Answer the following questions:

(a) In line 1, what is the case and number of *ovēs*?
(b) In line 2, what is the case and number of *filiō*?
(c) *dīxit* (line 3): put this verb into the plural.
(d) *discēdō* (line 3): put this verb into the imperfect.
(e) In line 4, *pāstōris filius* means 'the shepherd's son'. What is the Latin for 'the shepherds' sons'?
(f) In line 6, what part of which verb is *venīre*? Translate it.
(g) Identify and translate all the prepositions in this passage, together with the nouns they govern.
(h) In line 8, what would the opposite of *adsunt* be?

I'm afraid things don't look too jolly for the shepherd's son. Perhaps you already know what comes next; anyway, all will be revealed in due course.

The future tense: 1st conjugation

Meanwhile, to take your mind off our story, here's something completely different, something which we should greet with great joy; for it will make our stories much neater than they have hitherto been. Yes, here it comes in all its long awaited glory: the future tense. No longer must we 'decide to do' or 'desire to do' something or other. No! From now on, quite simply, we 'shall do' it. And who shall say us nay?

The future tense of *amō* (1st conjugation)		
1st person singular	*amābō*	I shall love
2nd person singular	*amābis*	you (singular) will love
3rd person singular	*amābit*	he, she or it will love
1st person plural	*amābimus*	we shall love
2nd person plural	*amābitis*	you (plural) will love
3rd person plural	*amābunt*	they will love

N.B.
(i) I hope you like this: it's as sonorous as the imperfect, and I particularly love that '*b*' in the middle of both tenses. I suggest you chant this aloud, over and over again, together and alone. And be sure to stress all those lovely long '*ā*'s.

(ii) I also hope you've noticed the smug correctness of my English above. This version (using 'shall' rather than 'will' in the 1st persons singular and plural) gives the simple future, or, as it used to be called in dusty old grammars, the 'future simple'. But if you replace 'shall' by 'will' or 'will' by 'shall', you have something much more emphatic, almost like a command; e.g. 'you shall do it' is more or less like 'you jolly well will do it'. On the subject of which, let us remember the sad story of the Frenchman who fell into a pond and cried out: 'Nobody shall save me. I will drown,' whereupon his would-be rescuers left him to it. Thus his failure to distinguish between his 'shalls' and his 'wills' cost him his life, poor man.

Exercise 1.8

Write out in full, as with *amō* above, the future tense of:

1. *laudō*
2. *nāvigō*
3. *rogō*
4. *festīnō*
5. *spectō*
6. *vocō*

Exercise 1.9

Translate into English:

1. *laudābit*
2. *nāvigābimus*
3. *rogābunt*
4. *festīnābit*
5. *spectābis*
6. *laudābō*
7. *nāvigō*
8. *rogābitis*
9. *festīnāmus*
10. *spectābimus*
11. *aedificābitis*
12. *habitābunt*
13. *labōrābit*
14. *oppugnābō*
15. *necābimus*
16. *portābunt*
17. *pugnant*
18. *spectābitis*
19. *superābō*
20. *vocābit*

Exercise 1.10

Translate into Latin:

1. He will praise.
2. They will hurry.
3. I shall watch.
4. You (pl.) will praise.
5. They will love.
6. We shall sing.
7. She will fight.
8. They will sail.
9. I shall ask.
10. You (sing.) will not fight.
11. The sailors will fight.
12. The girls will sing.
13. The masters will hurry.
14. They will praise the poets.
15. We shall watch the farmers.
16. The gods will attack the town.
17. Romulus will build a wall.
18. Romulus will kill Remus.
19. Romulus is killing Remus.
20. Romulus has killed Remus.

The future tense: 2nd conjugation

And here's the future of *moneō* (2nd conjugation). I'm sure you've worked it out already. However, here it is:

The future tense of *moneō* (2nd conjugation)		
1st person singular	*monēbō*	I shall warn, advise
2nd person singular	*monēbis*	you (singular) will warn, advise
3rd person singular	*monēbit*	he, she or it will warn, advise
1st person plural	*monēbimus*	we shall warn, advise
2nd person plural	*monēbitis*	you (plural) will warn, advise
3rd person plural	*monēbunt*	they will warn, advise

Exercise 1.11

Write out in full, as with *moneō,* the future tense of:

1. *dēleō*
2. *rīdeō*
3. *habeō*
4. *iubeō*
5. *respondeō*
6. *videō*

Exercise 1.12

Translate into English:

1.	*dēlēbunt*	11.	*monēbunt*
2.	*iubēbis*	12.	*habēbis*
3.	*terrēbit*	13.	*respondēbō*
4.	*habēbō*	14.	*tenent*
5.	*iubēbitis*	15.	*iubēbant*
6.	*terrēbuntne?*	16.	*vidēbās*
7.	*respondēbunt*	17.	*spectābunt*
8.	*tenēbimus*	18.	*dēlēbitis*
9.	*iubēbit*	19.	*rīdēbimus*
10.	*vidēbō*	20.	*habēbunt*

Exercise 1.13

Translate into Latin:

1.	They will have	11.	Will they be afraid?
2.	I shall warn	12.	I shall not reply
3.	She will hold	13.	You (sing.) will have
4.	We shall reply	14.	You (sing.) will not have
5.	They will terrify	15.	We shall fear
6.	He will have	16.	You (sing.) will hold
7.	We shall laugh	17.	They were ordering
8.	You (pl.) will see	18.	We shall not warn
9.	I shall hold	19.	It will have
10.	They will not terrify	20.	I do not see

Exercise 1.14

Translate into English:

1. *crās cum comitibus ad agrōs festīnābō.*
2. *posteā mīlitēs oppidum oppugnābunt.*
3. *rēgem et rēgīnam laudābimus.*
4. *dux mīlitēs pugnāre iubēbit.*
5. *mox puerī clāmābunt, sed puellae cantābunt.*
6. *terrēbuntne nōs iuvenēs clāmōribus?*
7. *puerī perterritī magistrō nōn respondēbunt.*
8. *mātrēs fīliīs cibum parābunt.*
9. *hodiē rēx poētīs aurum dabit.* *
10. *crās puella mātrem vidēbit.*

> Vocabulary
> *crās* = tomorrow
> *posteā* = afterwards
> *celeriter* = quickly
> *herī* = yesterday
> *hodiē* = today
> *tum* = then
> *nunc* = now

* N.B. The future of *dō* is *dăbō, dăbis, dăbit* etc., with that short 'ă' we had cause to mention in Book 1.

And for a bonus mark, in sentence 8 above, how can we know whether we are dealing with sons or daughters? You may need to refer back to Book 1, page 25, to answer this.

Exercise 1.15

Translate into Latin:

1. The fathers will order (their)* sons to read books.
2. He will love (his)* sister.
3. The inhabitants will remain in the town today.
4. The soldiers will praise their leader.
5. Soon the sailors will sail to the island.
6. The young men will laugh tomorrow in the fields.
7. I shall warn the men about the soldiers.
8. You (pl.) will hurry quickly from the town.
9. We shall not fear the shouts of the young men.
10. Will the angry old men frighten the women?

* Note that, in Latin, possessive adjectives ('my', 'your', 'his', 'her', 'its', 'our', 'their') are only used if the sense would not be clear without them, or for emphasis.

Exercise 1.16

Match up the following Latin words (1-8) with the English words (a-h) which are derived from them. Give the meaning of the Latin ones, and explain the connexion between these and the English words derived. e.g. 1 + d: *virtūs* = courage; courage is a type of manly virtue.

1.	*virtūs*	(a)	vocal
2.	*iuvenis*	(b)	military
3.	*rēx*	(c)	fraternal
4.	*mīles*	(d)	virtue
5.	*frāter*	(e)	senile
6.	*senex*	(f)	regal
7.	*pater*	(g)	juvenile
8.	*vōx*	(h)	paternal

3rd declension, neuter

And here's something else about 3rd declension nouns. We've had masculine ones, we've had feminine ones, we've had common ones. But what about neuters? Yes, there are plenty of these too, and this is how some of them go:

nōmen, nōminis, n. = 'name'		
	Singular	**Plural**
Nominative	*nōmen*	*nōmina*
Vocative	*nōmen*	*nōmina*
Accusative	*nōmen*	*nōmina*
Genitive	*nōminis*	*nōminum*
Dative	*nōminī*	*nōminibus*
Ablative	*nōmine*	*nōminibus*

N.B.

(i)   Two of the special features of neuter nouns (of whichever declension) can be seen here:

    (a) The vocative and accusative, singular and plural, are always the same as the nominative.

    (b) The nominative, vocative and accusative plural always end in a short '*a*'.

(ii) The ablative singular of *nōmen*, i.e. *nōmine,* means 'by name', i.e. 'called'.

e.g. *hīc est amīca mea, nōmine Claudia* = 'Here is my friend, called (lit. 'by name') Claudia.'

Exercise 1.17

Write out in full the following nouns, both of which go like *nōmen*:

1.   *flūmen, flūminis,* n. = river
2.   *iter, itineris,* n. = journey

(This last is a weird one, but it does help us to spell the word itinerary, so that's a bonus!)

Exercise 1.18

Translate into English:

1.   *tum puer, nōmine Mārcus, ad flūmen ambulāvit.*
2.   *nautae crās ad īnsulam nāvigābunt.*
3.   *hodiē iter facere cōnstituī.*
4.   *quis nōmen nōn habet?*
5.   *flūmina et agrōs semper amābō.*
6.   *rēgēs dē ducibus monēbimus.*
7.   *comitēs ducis itinera fēcērunt.*
8.   *dominus uxōrem vocābat.*
9.   *herī mātrem vīdimus.*
10. *posteā celeriter in oppidum festīnābimus.*

Exercise 1.19

Translate into Latin (with some easy ones thrown in):

1.   The queen loves the maid-servants.
2.   The teachers were praising the little boys.
3.   The good girls used to call the slaves.
4.   We do not like savage teachers.
5.   The wicked sailors are killing many inhabitants.
6.   The king's generals will fight bravely.
7.   We shall sail along the rivers.
8.   Who will reply to the leader?
9.   The old men often used to make journeys.
10. The youths will have many companions.

Exercise 1.20

And here's the continuation of our story, with great promptitude. Read the following passage carefully and answer the questions on it.

Wolf! Wolf! A false alarm

1   *pāstōris* fīlius <u>noctū</u> nōn dormiēbat, sed semper agrōs
     spectābat. subitō ventum audīvit saevum; '<u>lupus</u> adest!'
     clāmāvit, '<u>lupus</u>!' et magnā vōce <u>pāstōrēs</u> vocāvit.
     <u>pāstōrēs</u> dormiēbant, sed ubi iuvenis clāmōrem
5   audīvērunt, ad <u>stabulum</u> iuvenis celeriter cucurrērunt.
     <u>totum</u> <u>stabulum</u> <u>investīgāvērunt</u>, sed <u>lupus</u> aberat.
     tandem discessērunt <u>pāstōrēs</u>, et fīlius <u>pāstōris</u> iterum
     <u>sōlus</u> erat et agrōs spectābat.

pāstor, pāstōris, m. = shepherd.
noctū = by night
lupus, lupī, m. = wolf
stabulum, stabulī, n. = stable
tōtus, -a, -um (irregular) = whole
investīgō, -āre, -āvī, -ātum. Can you work this one out?!
sōlus, -a, -um (irregular) = alone

1.   Answer the following questions:

(a) In lines 1-2, why did the shepherd's son not sleep?
(b) In line 2, what made him think a wolf was there?
(c) In line 4, what were the other shepherds doing when the shepherd's son called out?
(d) In line 5, what did they promptly do?
(e) In line 6, which word tells us that they found no wolf. Translate this word.
(f) In line 7, which word tells us that they spent a long time in the stable? Translate this word.
(g) In line 8, which word makes us feel especially sorry for the shepherd's son. Translate this word.
(h) In line 8, what did the shepherd's son do after the other shepherds had gone?

2.   Translate the passage with foreboding. (Do you know this word?)

3.   Answer the following questions:

(a) In line 1, what is the present tense of *dormiēbat*?
(b) In line 1, if we wanted to put *agrōs* into the singular, what would we write?
(c) In line 2, what is the future of *spectābat*?
(d) In line 2, if we wanted to put *ventum saevum* into the plural, what would we write?
(e) In line 2, what is the plural of *adest*?
(f) In line 3, in which tense are *clāmāvit* and *vocāvit*? What would they be in the plural?
(g) *iuvenis* (line 4): give the dative singular and the dative plural of this noun.
(h) *cucurrērunt* (line 5): give the 1st person singular, present tense of this verb.

Vocabulary 1

In Latin Prep 1, we set out twenty new words in each chapter, thus collecting together the two hundred words required by the syllabus. In Latin Prep 2 we are only required to learn another one hundred and thirty or forty new words; so we shall have a list of around fifteen new words at the end of each chapter. These should be neatly collected together as we go along. And remember to learn all the details about each word, as we give them here.

Vocabulary 1

clāmor, clāmōris, m. = a shout
comes, comitis, c. = companion
coniūnx, coniugis, m/f. = husband/wife
dux, ducis, c. = leader, general, captain
homō, hominis, c. = human being, man/woman
iuvenis, iuvenis, c. = young person
mīles, mīlitis, c. = soldier

rēx, rēgis, m. = king
errō, -āre, -āvī, -ātum = I wander
nārrō, -āre, -āvī, -ātum = I tell
nūntiō, -āre, -āvī, -ātum = I announce
cārus, -a, -um = dear
longus, -a, -um = long
mortuus, -a, -um = dead

N.B.
(i)   *iuvenis* is generally masculine, meaning a 'youth' or 'young man'.
(ii)   *nārrō* means 'I tell' only in the sense 'I relate' (not 'I order').

I hope you have survived this first chapter.

Chapter 2

Pronouns: ego and tū

Remember the pronouns 'you' and 'I'? Hm! There we are, getting it wrong right from the word 'go'. I'm afraid the Romans had no 'nonsense' about thinking that 'you' are more important than 'I'. For them it was 'I' and 'you'. So, having already learnt these pronouns in the nominative and accusative in Latin Prep 1, we are now going to have them in full.

Pronouns (singular)
ego and *tū*

Nominative	*ego*	= I	*tū*	= you (singular)	
Accusative	*mē*	= me	*tē*	= you (singular) as the object	
Genitive	*meī*	= of me	*tuī*	= of you (singular)	
Dative	*mihi*	= to, for me	*tibi*	= to, for you (singluar)	
Ablative	*mē*	= by, with, from me	*tē*	= by, with, from you (singular)	

N.B.

(i) The genitives *meī* and *tuī* are rare, and we shall not be using them yet.
The final '*i*' of *mihi* and of *tibi* can be long or short. Now that we've told you this, we shall not be marking it.

(ii) We are saving up an exciting note on 'with me' and 'with you', so we shall not be using them for the moment. But all will soon be told.

(iii) In English we often omit the 'to' of the dative. For example, we often say 'give the boy a book', instead of 'give a book *to the boy*'; or 'I shall give Marcus a sword', instead of 'I shall give a sword *to Marcus*'. In Latin, we must not omit the 'to', and must always use the dative case whenever the sense requires it.

e.g. 'Give the boy a book!' = *dā puerō librum!*

'I shall give Marcus a sword.' = *Mārcō gladium dabō.*

This is particularly common with pronouns: e.g. 'Give me food!' is *dā mihi cibum!* and 'I gave you wine' is *tibi vīnum dedī.*

Exercise 2.1

Translate into English:

1. *puerōrum validōrum mihi nōmina dīc.*
2. *quid tibi mīles nūntiāvit?*
3. *ducem dē tē monēbō.*
4. *puellae mihi clāra verba cantābant.*
5. *uxor tibi auxilium dabit.*
6. *cūr rēgem dē mē monuistī?*
7. *Laelia mihi multa verba dīxit.*
8. *Mārcus ad tē festīnābit.*
9. *Quīntus dē flūminibus scrīpsit.*
10. *tē in oppidō manēre iubēbō.*

Exercise 2.2

Translate into Latin:

1. She will sing about me.
2. We shall warn the teacher about you, Quintus.
3. They have told* you (sing.) the boy's name. (*Use *dīcō* here.)
4. Oh! king, the boys will give you a big book.
5. Laelia, you will stay here, but I shall enter the temple.
6. We shall soon call you, mother.
7. The slave said 'Give me a good master!'
8. Master, shall I prepare you (some) food?
9. Write me many words, Aulus!
10. Marcus will hurry to me tomorrow.

Adjectives and 3rd declension nouns

Remember how dangerous it was to expect adjectives in *'-us'* always to rhyme with their nouns? We have already learnt to cope with the joys of *puer bonus*, and *agricolae bonī*, but this sort of thing is more dangerous still where such adjectives agree with 3rd declension nouns; for here they hardly ever rhyme. e.g. *bonī rēgēs* or *cum mīlite validō*; here the adjectives are agreeing with their nouns in gender, case and number, but they are clearly not rhyming. There will be very many more examples of this fearful danger, so beware.

Exercise 2.3

Make *bonus* agree with the following nouns, in gender, case and number, and translate.
e.g.   *rēgis bonī* = of the good king.

1. *rēgem*
2. *rēgēs* (nom.)
3. *ducis*
4. *comitum*
5. *cum mīlitibus*
6. *coniūnx* (fem.)
7. *hominem* (masc.)
8. *clāmōrī*
9. *rēgum*
10. *cum iuvene*
11. *comitēs* (nom.)
12. *comitēs* (acc.)
13. *vōx*
14. *lūcem*
15. *senem*
16. *virtūtem*
17. *mulierum*
18. *uxōrum*
19. *mātrēs* (voc.)
20. *sorōrī*

Exercise 2.4

Translate into English:

1. *bonī ducēs.*
2. *pulchrae mulierēs.*
3. *ad parvum frātrem.*
4. *ad saevōs.*
5. *rēgum amīcī saepe fessī senēs sunt.*

6. *puerī in lūce clārā stābunt.*
7. *ego et tū in agrō lūsimus.*
8. *laetī frātrēs comitum virtūtem laudābant.*
9. *malī fīliī patrem īrātum habent.*
10. *bonī fīliī laetō patrī cārī sunt.*

Exercise 2.5

Translate into English:

1. *bonī ducēs bonōs mīlitēs dūcunt.*
2. *pulchrae mulierēs in oppidō habitant.*
3. *parvae puellae frātrem validum habent.*
4. *incolae saevōs iuvenēs timēbant.*
5. *virtūtem magnam mīlitum laudābis.*

6. *lūcem clāram senēs timēbant.*
7. *fīlius malus rēgis incolās terruit.*
8. *mīlitēs validī patriam dēfendērunt.*
9. *dux valide, cūr oppidum parvum nōn oppugnās?*
10. *ego et tū mātrem pulchram habēmus.*

Exercise 2.6

Translate into Latin:

1. Bad soldiers will fear a good general.
2. We wish to have a strong king.
3. The wretched women fear the savage leader.
4. The well-known brothers have a beautiful sister.
5. A happy king's* slaves are happy.
6. He will have a crowd of many companions.
7. Marcus, you and I will see great generals.
8. The boys will sail along a deep river.
9. Young men will not fear wretched old men.
10. Will the angry husband frighten his beautiful wife?

*Here's a nice little note: *rēgis* = 'of a king' (from *rēx*); *rĕgis* = 'you (sing.) rule' (from *regō*). Good old quantities, eh?

More 3rd declension neuter nouns

Here are two more neuter nouns of the 3rd declension, which go like *nōmen*.

vulnus, vulneris, n. = wound
corpus, corporis, n. = body

These two are a bit worrying; they both end in '-*us*', but they are not 2nd declension like *dominus*. Their genitives singular, ending in '-*is*', show that they are 3rd declension. There are many neuter 3rd declension nouns like these two. And beware: some have their genitive singular in '-*eris*' and some have it in '-*oris*'.

mare = the sea

And while we're looking at 3rd declension neuter nouns, here's one more to keep us busy; we'll give it in full as it's such a very important word.

	Singular	Plural
mare, maris, n. = 'sea'		
Nominative	*mare*	*maria*
Vocative	*mare*	*maria*
Accusative	*mare*	*maria*
Genitive	*maris*	–
Dative	*marī*	*maribus*
Ablative	*marī*	*maribus*

N.B.

(i)   The ablative singular of *mare* regularly ends in '-*ī*', and is found in the wonderful little phrase: *terrā marīque* = 'by land and by sea.' (For this use of -*que* = 'and', see page 53.)

(ii) The nominative and accusative plural of *mare* ends '-*ia*', with an extra '*i*' popped in.

(iii) The genitive plural of *mare* is all but non-existent.

The Romans regarded the Mediterranean as their own property; they called it '*mare nostrum*'.

Exercise 2.7

Translate into English:

1.   *in marī multae īnsulae sunt.*
2.   *magnī hominēs magna corpora habent.*
3.   *ego flūmina amō, sed amīcus meus mare amat.*
4.   *maria, quod magna sunt, magnopere timeō.*
5.   *mīlitēs in proeliīs multa vulnera habēbant et dabant.*
6.   *senum corpora saepe fessa sunt.*
7.   *'ubi est mare nostrum?' rogāvit puer parvus. 'dīc mihi.'*
8.   *multī mīlitēs vulnera nōn timent.*

Exercise 2.8

Translate into Latin:

1.   They do not wish to give the boy a wound.
2.   The bodies of the farmers are strong.
3.   The sailors will sail in the sea.
4.   Give (pl.) me three spears and four swords.
5.   The Roman said: 'The Mediterranean* is great and beautiful.'
6.   We shall give you (sing.) water and wine.
7.   The king has a clear voice.
8.   The youths are dear to their mothers.

*What did the Romans call this sea? (see above).

Exercise 2.9

Read the following passage carefully and answer the questions on it.

Wolf! Wolf! A sad end

1   *iuvenis agrōs spectābat; subitō <u>lūna</u> fuit et <u>umbrās</u> vīdit*
    <u>arborum</u>. 'lupī adsunt!' clāmāvit, 'lupī!' et magnā vōce
    <u>pāstōrēs</u>, <u>quī</u> dormiēbant, vocāvit. vēnērunt <u>pāstōrēs</u>, et
    <u>stabulum</u> iterum <u>investīgāvērunt</u>, sed <u>lupī</u> aberant. mox
5   *discessērunt īrātī; iuvenis sōlus erat. subitō longās*
    <u>umbrās</u> vīdit et saevōs clāmōrēs audīvit. 'lupī adsunt!'
    clāmāvit, 'lupī!' et magnā vōce <u>pāstōrēs</u> iterum et
    iterum vocāvit; sed <u>pāstōrēs</u> rīsērunt et in <u>lectīs</u>
    mānsērunt; et <u>lupī</u> <u>ovēs</u> cōnsūmpsērunt et iuvenem.

lūna, -ae, f. = moon
umbra, -ae, f. = shadow
arbor, arbŏris, f. = tree
pāstor, pāstōris, m. = shepherd
quī = who
stabulum, -ī, n. = stable
investīgō, -āre, -āvī, -ātum = as
   before! (See page 14)
lectus, -ī, m. = bed
ovis, ovis, f. = sheep

1.   Answer the following questions:

    (a) In line 1, what enabled the young man to see shadows?
    (b) In line 2, what did he think they were shadows of?
    (c) In lines 3-4, what did the shepherds do when they arrived?
    (d) In line 4, which words tell us that there were no wolves? Translate these words.
    (e) In line 4, which word tells us that the shepherds spent less time in the stable than before?
        Translate this word.
    (f) In line 5, which word tells us what the shepherds felt about it all? Translate this word.
    (g) In lines 8-9, what did the shepherds do when they heard the young man cry again?
    (h) In line 9, what happened to the young man and the sheep?

2.   Translate the passage sorrowfully.

3.   Answer the following questions:

    (a) In line 1, what would *spectābat* be in the future tense?
    (b) In line 2, what are the case and number of *arborum*?
    (c) In line 5, if there had been only one shepherd, what would *discessērunt* have been?
    (d) In line 5, if there had been only one shepherd, what would *īrātī* have been?
    (e) In lines 5-6, what are the case and number of *longās umbrās*?
    (f) In line 8, what would *rīsērunt* be in the future?
    (g) In line 9, what would *mānsērunt* be in the imperfect?
    (h) In line 9, what would *iuvenem* be in the ablative plural?

nōs and vōs

When you've got over this story, here's something less harrowing. We've already learnt *ego* and *tū* in full. So here are their plurals, *nōs* and *vōs,* also in full:

	nōs = 'we'; *vōs* = 'you'	
Nominative	*nōs* = we	*vōs* = you
Accusative	*nōs* = us	*vōs* = you
Genitive	*nostrī / nostrum* = of us	*vestrī / vestrum* = of you
Dative	*nōbīs* = to us	*vōbīs* = to you
Ablative	*nōbīs* = by, with, from us	*vōbīs* = by, with, from you

N.B. The forms *nostrum* and *vestrum* as genitives of *nōs* and *vōs* are quite common in the sense *ūnus nostrum* = 'one of us', or *quis vestrum?* = 'which of you?' (literally who of you?) These genitives are called 'partitive' because *ūnus* or *quis* refers only to a part of 'us' or 'you'. The other forms (*nostrī* and *vestrī*) are called objective genitives, and we can leave these alone for now.

And now for our exciting note, promised earlier.

If you wish to say 'with me', 'with you (sing.)', 'with us', or 'with you (pl.)', you put *cum* (= 'with') *after* the pronoun in the ablative, and treat the whole thing as one word.

Thus: 'with me' = *mēcum*   'with us' = *nōbīscum*
          'with you (sing.)' = *tēcum*   'with you (pl.)' = *vōbīscum*

Exercise 2.10

Translate into English:

1. *mēcum ad oppidum festīnābunt.*
2. *tēcum lūdere cupiō.*
3. *quis nōbīscum nāvigābit?*
4. *malī hominēs nōs terrēbant.*
5. *dabitisne nōbīs gladiōs et hastās?*
6. *'vōbīscum,' dīxit magister, 'crās ambulābō.'*
7. *bonī mīlitēs vōbīs auxilium dabunt.*
8. *multī hominēs mē nōn laudant.*
9. *nōs hīc sumus; vōs ibi estis.*
10. *nūntius ad nōs cucurrit.*

Exercise 2.11

Translate into Latin:

1. They will hurry with you (pl.) to us.
2. Give us (some) food, master!
3. The savage soldiers will frighten us.
4. Who is coming with us to the good king?
5. The strong horse is running to you (pl.).
6. Many people[1] will fight with me and with you (sing.).
7. We shall stay here; you (pl.) will walk to the fields.
8. Who will prepare the food for us?
9. The good leaders will give you (pl.) help.
10. Oh! Publius, tell[2] me the king's name.

Notes:
[1] Either use *homō* or omit altogether.
[2] Use *dīcō.*

Exercise 2.12

Of which English words do the following Latin ones remind you? Explain the connexion between the Latin words and the English words that you choose.

1.	*mare*		4.	*nārrō*
2.	*corpus*		5.	*māter*
3.	*vulnus*		6.	*nōmen*

hic, haec, hoc

And now comes something very special. Lots and lots of people who know practically no Latin at all seem to know this. Or should I say, know 'this'?

hic, haec, hoc = 'this'

Singular

	Masculine	**Feminine**	**Neuter**
Nominative	*hic*	*haec*	*hoc*
Accusative	*hunc*	*hanc*	*hoc*
Genitive	*huius*	*huius*	*huius*
Dative	*huic*	*huic*	*huic*
Ablative	*hōc*	*hāc*	*hōc*

N.B.

(i) *huius* was originally spelt *huiius*, the two '*i*'s being consonantal, like two English 'y's, as in 'y-yes'! Although one of the '*i*'s was dropped in the spelling, they should both be pronounced, i.e. lingered on; the '*u*' before them is not long by nature and should not be pronounced as such. This characteristic is true of nearly all words where a letter '*i*' stands between two short vowels, as we shall soon see. e.g. *Troia* (= 'Troy') is really *Troiia*.

(ii) The '*ui*' of *huic* is a very rare diphthong; it should more or less rhyme with the '*ui*' in the English word 'quick'.

(iii) Remember to make *hic* agree with the noun it is describing.

e.g. *hic liber* = 'this book'; *haec īnsula* = 'this island'; *hoc bellum* = 'this war'.

(iv) *hic* alone often means 'he', i.e. 'this (man)'; similarly *haec* alone could mean 'she' and *hoc* alone would mean 'it'.

HIC, HAEC, HOC

Exercise 2.13

Make *hic* agree with the following nouns, and then translate into English.
e.g. *haec puella* = 'this girl.'

1. *oppidum* (nom.)
2. *puellam* (acc.)
3. *māter* (nom.)
4. *virō* (dat.)
5. *magistrī* (gen.)
6. *nautae* (dat.)
7. *templum* (acc.)
8. *vīnum* (nom.)
9. *agricola* (nom.)
10. *puerum* (acc.)

Exercise 2.14

Translate into English:

1. *in oppidum mēcum et cum hōc puerō festīnā!*
2. *hanc puellam cantāre iubēbō.*
3. *huius* māter bona mulier est.*
4. *huic virō gladium dedī.*
5. *dīc mihi huius magistrī nōmen.*
6. *nautae ab hōc oppidō discessērunt.*
7. *hoc templum mox vidēbō.*
8. *hoc vīnum validum est et bonum.*
9. *hic agricola in agrō labōrābit.*
10. *haec fēmina hunc virum amat.*

* *huius* alone could mean either 'his' or 'her', depending on the context.

Exercise 2.15

Translate into Latin:

1. I shall hurry to the town with this boy.
2. This woman's daughter is beautiful.
3. You (sing.) will give water to this soldier.
4. Have you (pl.) seen this girl?
5. She is good; he also is good.
6. We shall remain in this city.
7. They were running into this temple.
8. We shall sail from this island.
9. Will you (pl.) see this field?
10. They saw this man's son.

Exercise 2.16

Read the following passage carefully and anwer the questions on it.

Ibycus and the cranes

1	erat ōlim poēta Graecus, nōmine Ībycus; hic iter faciēbat; subitō malī hominēs pecūniam Ībycī cēpērunt et hunc necāre cōnstituērunt. subitō <u>gruēs</u> per caelum <u>volāvērunt</u>; et Ībycus, ubi <u>gruēs</u> vīdit, '<u>gruēs</u>,' dīxit, '<u>quae</u>
5	per caelum <u>volant</u>, hoc <u>facinus</u> oppidī incolīs nūntiābunt.' deinde malī hominēs poētam necāvērunt et in oppidum vēnērunt; et subitō per caelum <u>volāvērunt</u> gruēs. '<u>ēn</u>!' clāmāvit ūnus hominum amīcīs suīs, '<u>gruēs</u> hīc sunt, <u>quae</u> <u>facinus</u> nostrum, <u>ut</u> dīxit Ībycus, incolīs
10	oppidī nūntiābunt.' huius verba audīvērunt incolae et statim hunc cum amīcīs <u>pūnīvērunt</u>.

grūs, gruis, f. = crane (a type of bird)
volō, -āre, -āvī, -ātum = I fly
facinus, -ŏris, n. = crime
quae, f. = who
ēn = lo! behold!
ut (here) = as
pūniō, -īre, -īvī, -ītum = I punish

1. Answer the following questions in full:

   (a) In line 1, who was Ibycus?
   (b) In lines 1-2, what was he doing when the robbers met him?
   (c) In line 3, what did the robbers decide to do?
   (d) In lines 3-4, what did Ibycus see just before he died?
   (e) In lines 4-6, what did he prophesy?
   (f) In lines 7-8, what happened suddenly after the men had come to the town?
   (g) In lines 8-10, how would you rate the intelligence of the man who shouted 'ēn...'?
   (h) In line 9, which words revealed the men's guilt beyond doubt?
   (i) In lines 10-11, how was Ibycus' prophecy fulfilled? Answer in full.

2.   Translate the passage punitively.

3.   Answer the following questions:

(a) In line 1, what is the case of *nōmine* and what does it mean?
(b) In line 1, what is the case of *iter* and why is it in this case?
(c) In line 2, if, instead of 'Ibycus' money', we wanted to say 'this money', how would we change *pecūniam Ībycī*?
(d) In line 4, what would *volāvērunt* become in the future?
(e) In line 5, what is the case of *hoc facinus*? Why is this case used?
(f) In line 7, which tense of which verb is *vēnērunt*? And what does it mean?
(g) In line 10, what is the case of *huius*? What does it mean here?
(h) In line 10, if, instead of 'heard' we wanted to say 'are hearing', what would *audīvērunt* become?

Exercise 2.17

Translate into Latin:

1.   The farmers are warning the sailors.
2.   The good teacher was praising the good girls.
3.   Wicked boys are frightening our horses.
4.   The tired inhabitants were watching the long road.
5.   The beautiful girls were announcing good words.
6.   The soldiers will wander through the town with us.
7.   Will the leaders give help to the old men?
8.   We shall give our brother (some) books.
9.   You (pl.) will soon see this city.
10.   He will sing in the temple with me.

hic: plural

And let us end this chapter with the plural of *hic, haec, hoc*:

Plural			
	Masculine	**Feminine**	**Neuter**
Nominative	*hī*	*hae*	*haec*
Accusative	*hōs*	*hās*	*haec*
Genitive	*hōrum*	*hārum*	*hōrum*
Dative	*hīs*	*hīs*	*hīs*
Ablative	*hīs*	*hīs*	*hīs*

Apart from the neuter, nominative and accusative, this is almost embarrassingly straightforward; it's almost as if *hic* felt guilty about its weird singular. The meaning of 'this' in the plural is, of course, 'these'. Used alone, i.e. not in agreement with a noun, it would mean 'they', 'them' etc.

e.g.   *hī poētam necāvērunt* = 'they killed the poet.'
e.g.   *poēta hōs monuit* = 'the poet warned them.'

Exercise 2.18

Make *hic* agree with the following nouns, and then translate into English.
e.g. *hae puellae* = 'these girls'

1. *nautās*
2. *cum puellīs*
3. *oppida* (acc.)
4. *in agrīs*
5. *magistrī* (nom.)

6. *mulier*
7. *senēs* (nom.)
8. *mīlitum*
9. *iuvenum*
10. *rēgibus* (dat.)

Exercise 2.19

Translate into English:

1. *hī agricolae hōs nautās superābunt.*
2. *hī puerī cum hīs puellīs nōn pugnābunt.*
3. *hoc oppidum hōrum est.*
4. *in hīs agrīs multī equī habitant; hīs cibum dabō.*
5. *hic magister hās puellās laudābat.*
6. *huius māter mulier pulchra est.*
7. *librum huic senēs dedērunt.*
8. *haec bona sunt.*
9. *haec bona est.*
10. *hae undae saevae sunt.*

Exercise 2.20

Translate into Latin:

1. Will the master announce these words?
2. These horses will stand in the fields.
3. These men's slaves are present.
4. The boys praised these girls.
5. These women live in this town.
6. He was announcing good words; did you (pl.) hear them?
7. These books are his.
8. These books are theirs.
9. These bad men are fighting with these inhabitants.
10. Give (pl.) these soldiers these swords.

Vocabulary 2

Vocabulary 2

frāter, frātris, m. = brother	*Graecus, -a, -um* = Greek
pater, patris, m. = father	*vīvus, -a, -um* = alive
māter, mātris, f. = mother	*ruō, ruere, ruī, rutum* = I rush, charge (into)
soror, sorōris, f. = sister	*servō, -āre, -āvī, -ātum* = I save
senex, senis, m. = old man	*vincō, vincere, vīcī, victum* = I conquer
mare, maris, n. = sea	

What with 'this' and 'these', another chapter has sped away. It's still early days, though.

Chapter 3

The comparison of adjectives

It's ages since we've said anything about adjectives, and as there's rather a lot to get off my chest, we'd better start now with the comparison of adjectives, that is to say, comparatives and superlatives. When I was young, many centuries, if not millennia, ago, I was told that comparisons were odious. I don't think this was meant to refer to grammar, although it must be admitted that some Latin comparatives are not exactly lovable. However, we can forget about the nasty ones for the moment.

A comparative is 'more' something; if we want to say 'more kind' (kinder), or 'more angry' (angrier), we use the comparative of the adjectives 'kind' or 'angry'. To do this in Latin we chop off the '-us' of the adjective and add '-ior' to the stem.

e.g.   *laetus* = 'happy'; *laetior* = 'happier'.

A superlative is 'most' something; if we want to say 'most kind' or 'kindest', or 'most angry' or 'angriest', we use the superlative of the adjectives 'kind' or 'angry'. To do this in Latin we chop off the '-us' and add '-issimus' to the stem.

e.g.   *laetus* = 'happy'; *laetissimus* = 'most happy', 'happiest'.

To discover how these comparative and superlative adjectives decline, read on.

laetior = happier

Comparative adjectives decline as follows, using (as you can see) the endings of the 3rd declension.

laetior, laetius = 'happier'		
Singular		
	Masculine	**Feminine**	**Neuter**
Nominative	*laetior*	*laetior*	*laetius*
Vocative	*laetior*	*laetior*	*laetius*
Accusative	*laetiōrem*	*laetiōrom*	*laetius*
Genitive	*laetiōris*	*laetiōris*	*laetiōris*
Dative	*laetiōrī*	*laetiōrī*	*laetiōrī*
Ablative	*laetiōre*	*laetiōre*	*laetiōre*
Plural		
Nominative	*laetiōrēs*	*laetiōrēs*	*laetiōra*
Vocative	*laetiōrēs*	*laetiōrēs*	*laetiōra*
Accusative	*laetiōrēs*	*laetiōrēs*	*laetiōra*
Genitive	*laetiōrum*	*laetiōrum*	*laetiōrum*
Dative	*laetiōribus*	*laetiōribus*	*laetiōribus*
Ablative	*laetiōribus*	*laetiōribus*	*laetiōribus*

We have unleashed the whole of this on to you in one go, because it really is unexpectedly straightforward. The masculine and feminine are the same throughout and go exactly like 3rd declension nouns, adding on to themselves the regular 3rd declension case endings. The only really surprising thing is the neuter singular *laetius*. I admit that this *'-ius'* is certainly a weirdie as a neuter singular, but we must have something odd somewhere, mustn't we?

As for the superlative *laetissimus*, it is entirely straightforward. It goes exactly like *bonus* throughout.

Exercise 3.1

Give the comparative and superlative (nom. masc. sing.), plus meanings, of:

1.	*clārus*	5.	*altus*
2.	*saevus*	6.	*īrātus*
3.	*cārus*	7.	*longus*
4.	*nōtus*	8.	*laetus*

Than

Now that we can say 'more', we need to be able to say 'more than' something. There are two ways of doing this in Latin:

(i)   Either we use *quam* followed by the same case as that which precedes it (generally the nominative).

e.g.   *puella laetior est quam puer* = 'the girl is happier than the boy.'

(ii)   Or we use the ablative alone.

e.g.   *puer puellā laetior est* = 'the boy is happier than the girl.'

This second way is called an 'ablative of comparison' and is quite swanky if you wish to impress people.

Exercise 3.2

Translate into English:

1.   *vōx puerī clārior est quam vōx senis.*
2.   *nōn vīdī saeviōrēs mīlitēs.*
3.   *bonus magister puellae cārior est quam malus.*
4.   *quis hōc rēge nōtior est?*
5.   *maria altiōra sunt quam flūmina.*
6.   *puerī īrātiōrēs erant quam puellae.*
7.   *haec via nostrā longior est.*
8.   *nostrum templum nōtius est vestrō.*

Note:
(i)   The comparative alone in Latin sometimes means 'rather...' or 'too...'
        e.g. *hic liber longior est* = 'this book is rather long' or 'this book is too long'.
(ii)   The superlative sometimes means 'very'.
        e.g. *hic liber longissimus est* = 'this book is very long.'

Exercise 3.3

Translate into Latin:

1. Our sea* is deeper than your (sea).
2. The soldiers are too savage.
3. This sword is longer than this spear.
4. The river is deep, but the sea is deeper.
5. Who is dearer to me than my friend?
6. I have not seen a happier boy.
7. The old men are angrier than the youths.
8. The temple is higher than this wall.

*What did the Romans call the Mediterranean?

Exercise 3.4

Translate into English:

1. *quis ducum nōtissimus est?*
2. *vīdistīne clārissimam mulierem?*
3. *in hāc īnsulā haec via longissima est.*
4. *māter filiīs et filiābus cārissima est.*
5. *hī senēs īrātissimī sunt incolārum.*
6. *hoc vulnus altissimum est.*

Exercise 3.5

Translate into Latin:

1. Who is the angriest of the sailors?
2. This boy has a very well known father.
3. This woman is the most famous of the inhabitants.
4. This man will build a very high temple.
5. This soldier is very savage.
6. He is to me the dearest of my brothers.

N.B.

We've spared you this once so far, but you may well have guessed it. Quite a lot of very common words have irregular comparatives and superlatives, such as *bonus, malus, magnus, parvus* and *multus*. We shall deal with these later. By the way, have you noticed that it is these important words that tend to be the most irregular (like *sum* for example). I think that being so important goes to their heads and they start getting above themselves, having ideas of their own. It's no good complaining, though. And anyway, this tendency is by no means confined to Latin.

ille, illa, illud

Now that we've mastered *hic, haec, hoc* (= 'this'), we simply can't wait another minute before learning *ille, illa, illud* (= 'that').

ille, illa, illud = 'that'			
Singular			
	Masculine	**Feminine**	**Neuter**
Nominative	*ille*	*illa*	*illud*
Accusative	*illum*	*illam*	*illud*
Genitive	*illīus*	*illīus*	*illīus*
Dative	*illī*	*illī*	*illī*
Ablative	*illō*	*illā*	*illō*

The second '*i*' of the genitive is sometimes short. The dative, because it isn't so outlandish as the dative of *hic,* can very easily be got wrong, so be very, very careful with it. e.g. 'to that girl' = *illī puellae.* I need hardly point out the weirdness of the nominative and accusative neuter.

Exercise 3.6

Translate into English:

1. *ubi est illa puella?*
2. *hic puer laetior est illō.*
3. *ille senex īrātissimus est.*
4. *vīdistīne illam mulierem?*
5. *crās in illud oppidum festīnābimus.*
6. *librum dabō illī fēminae.*
7. *pugnābisne cum illō mīlite?*
8. *illīus pater nōtissimus est.*
9. *hic parvus nauta illō magnō saevior est.*
10. *magister illum puerum laudābit.*

Exercise 3.7

Translate into Latin:

1. This girl is happier than that one.
2. Watch that field, soldiers.
3. We shall hurry into that town with you (pl.).
4. Tomorrow I shall see that boy.
5. Will you sail along that river, sailors?
6. Marcus, give that teacher this book.
7. I gave that woman that book yesterday.
8. Is Quintus that girl's brother?
9. That farmer is Aulus' father.
10. I shall fight with that soldier tomorrow.

And now it's time for a new story.

Exercise 3.8

Read the following passage carefully, and answer the questions on it.

The Story of Croesus
King Croesus is not impressed by the philosopher, Solon

1   *Lȳdia magna terra fuit et multōs incolās habuit; rēgem*
habuit nōmine Croesum. ōlim <u>philosophus</u> <u>Solō</u> in
Lȳdiam iter fēcit; illum Croesus ad <u>rēgiam</u> suam vocāvit
et ostendit illī multam pecūniam et aurum multum; et
5   *<u>Solōnem</u> rogāvit 'quis in <u>orbe</u> terrārum vir*
<u>fortūnātissimus</u> est?' <u>bis</u> rogāvit illum; Solō tamen nōn
respondit 'tū es'. rēx igitur īrātissimus erat et dīxit
<u>Solōnī</u> 'ego magnus rēx sum, multōs hominēs regō,
multum aurum habeō; cūr nōn dīxistī mihi "tū hominum
10   *<u>fortūnātissimus</u> es"?' respondit <u>Solō</u> 'vir laetus <u>fortasse</u>*
nōn semper laetus <u>erit</u>; <u>nēmō</u> igitur <u>fortūnātus</u> est
<u>antequam</u> mortuus est.' ad hoc rīsit Croesus, <u>nec</u>
<u>Solōnem</u> laudāvit.

philosophus, -ī, m. =
  philosopher
Solō, Solōnis, m. = Solon, a
  famous Athenian lawgiver
  and philosopher
rēgia, -ae, f. = palace
orbis, orbis, m. = circle; *orbis*
  terrārum = the world
fortūnātus, -a, -um = fortunate
bis = twice
erit = will be
fortasse = perhaps
nēmō (irregular) = no one
antequam = before
nec = and not

1.   Answer the following questions:

   (a) In lines 1-2, who was Croesus?
   (b) In line 2 who was Solon?
   (c) In line 4, what did Croesus show Solon?
   (d) In lines 5-6, what question did Croesus ask Solon?
   (e) In lines 6-7, how did Solon respond?
   (f) In line 7, what did Croesus feel about this?
   (g) In lines 11-12, before what event did Solon say no one could be called fortunate?
   (h) In lines 10-11, why did he believe that this was the case?
   (i) In line 12, how did Croesus feel about this?
   (j) In lines 12-13, and how did he feel about Solon?

2.   Translate the passage philosophically.

3. Answer the following questions in full:

   (a) In line 2, what does *nōmine* come from?

   (b) In line 2, what is the case and number of *nōmine*?

   (c) In line 3, we are told that Solon 'made a journey'. If we wanted to say that he 'made journeys', what should we write instead of *iter fēcit*?

   (d) In lines 3-4, if Solon had been a woman, what change, if any, might we have to make (i) to *illum,* (ii) to *illī*?

   (e) In line 5, what is the case and number of *orbe*? And why is it in this case?

   (f) In line 7, put *respondit* into the plural.

   (g) In lines 7-8, we are told that the king 'said' to Solon. What would *dīxit* become if we wished to say the king 'was saying'?

   (h) In line 9, what is the case of *mihi*?

   (i) In line 9, put *tū* into the dative.

   (j) In line 11, mention anything special about *igitur*.

Notes:

(i)   Lydia is in Asia Minor.

(ii)   Note that Greek names ending in '-on' frequently drop the 'n' in Latin in the nominative and vocative but pick it up later. Thus *Platō, -ōnis,* the famous philosopher, whose name (in Greek) was *Platōn*.

(iii) Croesus and Solon lived in the 6th Century BC. This century went from 599 to 500. Just work it out, remembering that BC means Before Christ, and you'll see I'm not mad – yet. Incidentally, note that we pronounce the vowels in Solon's name the wrong way round, as we did with Romulus and Remus. In Latin he is *Sŏlō*, in English he is Sōlŏn.

(iv)   I've just discovered that there's a splendid Latin word, *philosopha*, used by Cicero for a female philosopher. I thought you'd like to know this, especially the girls among you.

(v)   In lines 11-12, Solon did not mean that one *would* be fortunate after dying, but that one could certainly not be *considered* so before, since anything might happen to one. The Greeks were not exactly optimistic!

ille: plural

Let us now return to *ille* and look at its plural, which is really insultingly regular; as if we couldn't cope with a weirdity or two! Or didn't even secretly enjoy them! Anyway, here it goes:

	illī, illae, illa = 'those'		
Plural			
	Masculine	**Feminine**	**Neuter**
Nominative	*illī*	*illae*	*illa*
Accusative	*illōs*	*illās*	*illa*
Genitive	*illōrum*	*illārum*	*illōrum*
Dative	*illīs*	*illīs*	*illīs*
Ablative	*illīs*	*illīs*	*illīs*

Exercise 3.9

Make *ille* agree with the following nouns, and then translate into English.
e.g. *illae puellae* = those girls

1. *mīlitēs* (nom.)
2. *ducēs* (acc.)
3. *librōrum*
4. *in templō*
5. *mulieribus* (dat.)

6. *incolās*
7. *comitum*
8. *equī* (gen.)
9. *rēx*
10. *mātrēs* (nom.)

Some more words, etc. (!)

We are now going to learn some new words, some of which need a bit of explanation.

(i) *cēterī* = 'the rest (of)'. We shall only be using this in the plural, which is far commoner than the singular. It has all three genders and goes like *miserī.*

e.g. *cēterī puerī* = 'the rest of the boys'; *cēterae puellae* = 'the rest of the girls'.

For the neuter plural you should remember our expression 'et cetera', pronounced as one English word and abbreviated as 'etc.' This expression (*et cētera)* really means 'and the rest of things', i.e. everything remaining.

(ii) *paucī* = 'few'. This is only found in the plural. It is entirely regular, with feminine *paucae* and neuter *pauca,* like the plural of *bonus.* 'Few' in English is opposed to 'many.' So 'few came' means 'not many came'; whereas 'a few came' means that although there weren't many, at least there were <u>some</u>. The Oxford Concise Dictionary sums it up beautifully, saying that 'few' is opposed to 'many', while 'a few' is opposed to 'none'. Just meditate on this. The Latin *paucī* can mean 'few' or 'a few'. It depends on our old friend, the context.

(iii) *medius, -a, -um,* is regular. Its general meaning 'middle (of)' is a little muddling, as the word is not followed by a genitive, as it is in English. For example *media īnsula* would mean 'the middle *of* the island'.

(iv) *sōlus, -a, -um* = 'alone'. This word is hopelessly mixed up. After starting quite innocently, it suddenly decides it wants to be like *ille.* One might have thought that this is the result of its being so much alone but unfortunately there are quite a few others who do the same thing, including *unus* = one.

sōlus, sōla, sōlum = 'alone'			
Singular			
	Masculine	**Feminine**	**Neuter**
Nominative	*sōlus*	*sōla*	*sōlum*
Accusative	*sōlum*	*sōlam*	*sōlum*
Genitive	*sōlīus*	*sōlīus*	*sōlīus*
Dative	*sōlī*	*sōlī*	*sōlī*
Ablative	*sōlō*	*sōlā*	*sōlō*

The '*i*' of the genitive can sometimes be short. The plural is as regular as that of *ille,* only less frequent than the singular.

Exercise 3.10

Translate into English:

1. *illī mīlitēs validī sunt; cēterī tamen nōn sunt.*
2. *illī paucī ducēs bellum gerere nōn cupiunt.*
3. *hōs paucōs librōs illīs puellīs date!*
4. *cēterae mulierēs aberant.*
5. *quis cum illīs puerīs in mediā viā stetit?*
6. *paucī mīlitēs illōs incolās līberābant.*
7. *pūnīvēruntne illī cēterōs puerōs?*
8. *illī equī in mediō agrō sunt.*
9. *rēx bonus illōs servōs līberābit et servābit.*
10. *cūr māter illārum puellārum abest?*

> **Vocabulary**
> *līberō, -āre, -āvī, -ātum* = I set free
> *salūtō, -āre, -āvī, -ātum* = I greet
> *gerō, gerere, gessī, gestum* = I carry on, do
> *bellum gerere* = to wage war
>   (this phrase is especially frequent.)
> *pūniō, -īre, -īvī, -ītum* = I punish

Exercise 3.11

Translate into Latin:

1. Who will give the rest of the spears to those soldiers?
2. I have set free those few women.
3. Those teachers have not punished the rest of the boys.
4. Where are those girls' books?
5. The good farmers will set free those few horses.
6. We shall greet those teachers in the middle of the city.
7. Why were those men punishing the rest of the inhabitants?
8. Sextus and Aulus will greet those few sailors.
9. Those men were standing in the middle of the street.
10. There are a few poets in the temple today.

Exercise 3.12

Translate into English:

1. *puer sōlus in agrō lūdēbat.*
2. *haec hasta Mārcī sōlīus est.*
3. *ūnum gladium habet et ūnam hastam.*
4. *illa verba rēgī sōlī nūntiā.*
5. *haec dōna ūnī puerō dedī.*
6. *illa puella sōla in templō cantābit.*
7. *cum ūnō virō in oppidum festīnābō.*
8. *in illā terrā ūnum sōlum flūmen est.*

Exercise 3.13

Translate into Latin:

1. The king alone was fighting.
2. The queen alone was happy.
3. He is the father of one girl alone.
4. We gave the books to that master alone.
5. We were fighting with that one soldier.
6. Laelia and Sulpicia gave those gifts to one woman.
7. Who will stay alone in the temple?
8. One boy built that wall around the temple.

The future of regō

The time has now come to introduce some more futures: I'm afraid that for some reason the lovely *-bō, -bis, -bit* endings no longer feature. Instead we have more austere parts, but at least they are the same for 3rd, 4th and mixed conjugations, so that's one thing. Anyway, here's the future of *regō*:

1st person singular	*regam*	I shall rule
2nd person singular	*regēs*	you (sing.) will rule
3rd person singular	*reget*	he/she/it will rule
1st person plural	*regēmus*	we shall rule
2nd person plural	*regētis*	you (plur.) will rule
3rd person plural	*regent*	they will rule

Note particularly how, after starting with '*-am*', it produces a rather feeble attempt to catch you out by changing to '*-ēs*' and '*-et*' and carries on like this right up to the end. The real trick here is that these *-ēs, -et, -ēmus, -ētis, -ent* endings look identical to the present tense of *moneō*, so beware.

Exercise 3.14

Translate into Latin:

1. We shall rule.
2. I shall lead.
3. She will conquer.
4. You (sing.) will read.
5. They will send.
6. We shall write.
7. I shall show.
8. He will fight.
9. You (pl.) will stand.
10. They will play.

The future of audiō and capiō

In the 4th conjugation, the endings '*-am*', '*-ēs*', '*-et*', etc. are added to the final '*i*' of the stem, producing *audiam*, etc. Similarly, the future of *capiō* is *capiam*.

1st person singular	*audiam*	*capiam*
2nd person singular	*audiēs*	*capiēs*
3rd person singular	*audiet*	*capiet*
1st person plural	*audiēmus*	*capiēmus*
2nd person plural	*audiētis*	*capiētis*
3rd person plural	*audient*	*capient*

Exercise 3.15

Set out in full the future tense of:

1. *dīcō*
2. *faciō*
3. *veniō*

4. *bibō*
5. *iaciō*
6. *dormiō*

Exercise 3.16

Translate into English:

1. *dux mīlitēs in proelium dūcet.*
2. *crās in oppidō dormiēmus.*
3. *bellumne mox gerētis?*
4. *posteā cibum cōnsūmēmus.*
5. *agricolae ad flūmen current.*

6. *Claudia et Sulpicia ex īnsulā discēdent.*
7. *Titus cum Pūbliō in agrō lūdet.*
8. *novumne librum scrībēs, Quīnte?*
9. *hic rēx illum rēgem vincet.*
10. *hunc librum nunc legam.*

Exercise 3.17

Translate into Latin:

1. Who will rule this land?
2. These boys will not eat this food.
3. Tomorrow I shall make a journey.
4. You (plur.) will rush into the sea.
5. Will they conquer those soldiers?

6. You (sing.) will carry three books into the temple.
7. The sailors will not wish to take that gold.
8. We shall hear the words of the leader.
9. What will they say to those savage soldiers?
10. Will those women always love those old men?

Exercise 3.18

Some easy sentences with some harder ones. Translate into Latin:

1. The boys are building a high wall.
2. The teachers are praising the good girls.
3. We are overcoming the wicked sailors.
4. The masters were warning the slaves.
5. You (sing.) were watching those big horses.

6. Who will wish to rule these inhabitants?
7. These women are very famous.
8. Those soldiers were very savage.
9. Sextus and Gnaeus will not fight with Cassia.
10. Quintus, the poet, has written many books.

Exercise 3.19

What English words do the following Latin ones remind you of? Explain the connexion between the Latin words and the English ones you have chosen.

1. *medius*
2. *sōlus*
3. *pūniō*
4. *līberō*
5. *servō**

*I'm afraid this might remind you of 'serve', but unfortunately that comes from a different Latin verb. Think instead of an English compound verb that means 'keep safe'.

Exercise 3.20

Read the following passage carefully, and answer the questions on it.

Croesus receives an oracular response

1   *Cȳrus Persārum rēx erat; ille semper validior erat et
     validior; Croesus cum illō bellum gerere cupīvit. nūntiōs
     igitur mīsit Delphōs; nam ibi ōrāculum Apollinis erat
     sacerrimum; illud habitābat sacerdōs nōtissima; per*
5   *hanc hominēs deus dē futūrō monēbat; et hominēs huic
     sacerdōtī crēdēbant. nūntiī igitur Croesī hanc
     rogāvērunt, 'dēbetne Croesus bellum cum Cȳrō gerere?'
     respondit illa 'magnum sīc imperium dēlēbit.' Croesus,
     ubi hoc audīvit, laetus erat et bellum gessit, sed vīcit*
10   *Cȳrus Croesum; et comprehendit Croesus verba
     sacerdōtis; nam imperium dēlēvit magnum: nōn tamen
     Cȳrī, ut expectāvit, imperium dēlēvit, sed suum.*

Persae, Persārum, m. pl. = the
   Persians
Delphī, -ōrum, m. pl. = Delphi
   (see below)
ōrāculum, -ī, n. = oracle
   (see below)
Apollō, -inis, m. = Apollo
sacerdōs, -ōtis, c. = priest or
   priestess
futūrum, -ī, n. = the future
crēdō, -ere, crēdidī, crēditum
   (+ dat.) = I believe
dēbeō, -ēre, dēbuī, dēbitum
   (+ infin.) = I ought, must
imperium, -ī, n. (here) = empire
comprehendō, -ere, comprehendī,
   comprehēnsum = I understand
ut (here) = as
exspectō, -āre, -āvī, -ātum =
   I expect, wait for

Notes:

(i)   Cyrus was a great and famous king of Persia from 559-529 BC; he is mentioned with much
       respect in the Old Testament.

(ii)   We have already met the great god, Phoebus Apollo, who was, among other things, the god of
       prophecy.

(iii) In Delphi, in central Greece, was the oracle of Apollo. This was a sacred place, where a priestess
       gave prophetic responses to questions about the future. These were believed to be true; but, as in
       the story above, they were often highly ambiguous! The site of Delphi is wonderfully beautiful.
       Note that, when going to or from towns or small islands, a preposition is not used.

1.   Answer the following questions:

   (a) In lines 1-2 why do you think Croesus wished to go to war with Cyrus?
   (b) In lines 2-3, what did Croesus do before going to war?
   (c) Why did he do this?
   (d) In lines 4-5, what was the importance of the priestess?
   (e) In line 8, to what does *sīc* refer?
   (f) If you had to choose an English adjective (other than ambiguous) to describe the oracle's response, what would it be?
   (g) In lines 8-9, why was Croesus pleased with the oracle's response?
   (h) In line 12, whose empire did Croesus destroy?

2.   Translate the passage thoughtfully.

3.   Answer the following questions:

   (a) In lines 1 and 2, what part of *validus* is *validior*?
   (b) What would its superlative be?
   (c) In line 2, from which verb does *gerere* come? Give its principal parts and meaning.
   (d) In line 2, from which verb does *cupīvit* come? Give its principal parts and meaning.
   (e) In line 5, what are the case and gender of *huic* here?
   (f) In lines 6-7, the messengers of Croesus asked the priestess a question. If we wanted to say 'Croesus asked her', what would *rogāvērunt* become?
   (g) In lines 9-10, we are told that Cyrus conquered Croesus. How would the verb *vīcit* change if we were to put it into the imperfect?
   (h) In line 11, put *dēlēvit* into the plural.

Vocabulary 3

Notes:
[1] Some nouns only exist in the plural.
[2] *in mediā viā* = 'in the middle *of* the street.' Note how the word for 'street' goes into the ablative, not the genitive, as in English.

We shall soon be *in mediō librō* if we go on like this.

Chapter 4

The pluperfect tense

You'd hardly have thought it possible, but we've got a completely new tense for you, one which we haven't mentioned before as such, and have hardly even hinted at. (I did say that there were lots and lots of treats in the offing!) This tense is the pluperfect and means 'had', e.g. 'I had loved'. Luckily it is formed in exactly the same way by all the conjugations.

	amāveram = 'I had loved'	
1st person singular	*amāveram*	I had loved
2nd person singular	*amāverās*	you (sing.) had loved
3rd person singular	*amāverat*	he, she, it had loved
1st person plural	*amāverāmus*	we had loved
2nd person plural	*amāverātis*	you (plur.) had loved
3rd person plural	*amāverant*	they had loved

The pluperfect is formed by removing the final *'i'* from the perfect (to get the perfect stem) and adding *'-eram'* etc. You will note that these pluperfect tense endings are none other than the imperfect of *sum*, so they are easy to learn. Thus the pluperfect of *moneō* is *monu-eram* that of *regō* is *rēx-eram*, of *audiō* is *audīv-eram* and of *capiō* is *cēp-eram*. No catches anywhere – completely straightforward. Note that the *'e'* of *amāvērunt* (perfect) is long, while the *'e'* of *amāverant* (pluperfect) is short.

The pluperfect tense is used to refer to something that *had* happened in the past (before actions described by the past or imperfect tense).

e.g. *rēgīna ancillās vocāvit, sed illae iam discesserant* =
'The queen called her maid-servants, but they had already departed.'

Exercise 4.1

Write out in full the pluperfect of the following verbs, as the pluperfect of *amō* is written above:

1. *festīnō*
2. *līberō*
3. *dēleō*
4. *videō*
5. *dormiō*
6. *faciō*

Exercise 4.2

Translate into English:

1. *rēxerat*
2. *cēperāmus*
3. *monuerant*
4. *ceciderat*
5. *lēgeram*
6. *rīserātis*
7. *lūserat*
8. *habitāveram*
9. *iusserant*
10. *ostenderāmus*

Exercise 4.3

Translate into Latin:

1.   He had warned
2.   We had ruled
3.   They had heard
4.   You (sing.) had captured
5.   She had said

6.   We had ordered
7.   You (pl.) had played
8.   They had attacked
9.   We had run
10. I had given

Exercise 4.4

Translate into English:

1.   *ubi in oppidum vēnimus, Gnaeus iam Rōmam discesserat.*
2.   *puellae librum dedī, sed illa hunc iam lēgerat.*
3.   *magister puerōs laudāvit; in templo bene cantāverant.*
4.   *servī laetī erant; nam dominus illōs līberāverat.*
5.   *illōs mīlitēs hī vīcērunt; hōs dux bonus dūxerat.*
6.   *illī hominēs fessī erant; longissimum iter fēcerant.*
7.   *Quīntus, poēta, sextum librum scrībēbat; iam quīnque librōs scrīpserat.*
8.   *cūr nōbīs mala verba dīxistī? illa iam saepe audīverāmus.*

Exercise 4.5

Translate into Latin:

1.   The slaves were wretched; for the master had not praised them.
2.   The generals gave the soldiers gifts; they had conquered the inhabitants of the town.
3.   We greeted the sailors; they had sailed to the island.
4.   The little boys were tired; for they had run into the temple.
5.   The king was very angry, slaves; for you had not worked in the fields.
6.   We were very happy; for we had seen our friend.
7.   Why did you not eat the food with us, Claudia? We had prepared it for you.
8.   We came into the town yesterday; for we had hurried.

More on comparatives and superlatives

A flashback now to comparatives and superlatives. I'm sure you remember *laetior, laetissimus* and others. Well, here are some different types, particularly of superlatives. They are formed from adjectives in '*-er*', and let's have the comparative first.

1.   Comparative
     To form the comparative, we add '*-ior*' to the stem of the adjective.
     (a) If the adjective goes like *miser*, retaining the '*e*', then the comparative will have an '*e*'.
         Thus, the comparative of *miser* is *miserior*.
     (b) But if the adjective drops its '*e*', then the comparative too will drop its '*e*'. Thus, the
         comparative of *pulcher* is *pulchrior*.

     The comparatives then decline like *laetior* (see page 27).

2. Superlative

    The superlatives of these adjectives in '*-er*' are quite different from the lovely '*-issimus*' forms that we already know. Instead, they add '*-rimus*' to the nominative, masculine singular, whether the '*e*' gets dropped or not. Thus, the superlative of *miser* is *miserrimus, -a, -um*; and the superlative of *pulcher* is *pulcherrimus, -a, -um*.

    These then decline as perfectly regular adjectives in '*-us*' and should give us no trouble.

Exercise 4.6

Give the comparative and superlative (nom. masc. sing.) of:

pulchra... pulchrior... pulcherrima

1. *pulcher*
2. *clārus*
3. *miser*
4. *longus*
5. *laetus*

Exercise 4.7

Translate into English:

1. *Sulpicia pulcherrima mulier est.*
2. *quis est pulchrior quam ego?*
3. *miserrimōs puerōs in viā vīdī.*
4. *hoc templum sacerrimum est.* *
5. *dā hoc dōnum pulcherrimae puellae.*
6. *quis est miserior quam ille?*
7. *ille incolārum miserrimus est.*
8. *vīdistīne miseriōrēs puellās?*

*Strangely enough, *sacer* and *sacerrimus* often mean their exact opposite, i.e. 'accursed'. The comparative does not appear to be used.

Exercise 4.8

Translate into Latin:

1. These women are more beautiful than those.
2. Where are the books of the more wretched girls?
3. What is more beautiful than this gift?
4. This temple stands in a most sacred place.
5. These boys are more wretched than those.
6. Oh! Marcus, give this food to a more wretched old man!
7. Laelia is the most beautiful of the inhabitants.
8. They give many books to the more beautiful daughter.

It's now time to return to the story of Croesus, whom we left in a distinctly unenviable state.

Exercise 4.9

Read the passage carefully and answer the questions on it.

The story of Croesus: his ultimate fate

1   *Cȳrus, ubi Croesum vīdit, mīlitēs suōs illum in <u>vincula</u>*
    iacere iussit; et hōs magnum <u>acervum</u> aedificāre <u>lignī</u> et
    ibi Croesum pōnere iussit; nam illum <u>incendere</u>
    cōnstituerat. subitō, 'ō Solō,' <u>ter</u> clāmāvit Croesus; rogat
5   *Cȳrus 'quis est Solō ille? et cūr illum vocās?' respondit*
    Croesus 'Solō <u>philosophus</u> Graecus est.' et dīxit Cȳrō
    Croesus verba Solōnis: 'nēmō <u>fortūnātus</u> est antequam
    mortuus est.' et statim Croesum līberāvit Cȳrus; et
    posteā semper illum comitem habēbat et amīcum.

vinculum, -ī, n. = chain
acervus, -ī, m. = pile, heap
lignum, -ī, n. = wood, esp.
    firewood
incendō, -ere, incendī,
    incēnsum = I burn (trans.)
ter = three times, thrice
fortūnātus, -a, -um = fortunate

1.   Answer the following questions:

(a) In lines 1-2, what did Cyrus do first when he saw Croesus?
(b) In lines 2-3, what did he then order his men to do?
(c) In lines 3-4, why did he do this?
(d) In line 4, what did Croesus do?
(e) In lines 4-5, what did Cyrus ask Croesus?
(f) In line 6, what did Croesus say about Solon?
(g) In lines 7-8, translate the words of Solon.
(h) In lines 8-9, what was the effect of these words on Cyrus?

2.   Translate the passage happily. You never thought (did you?) that the story would end happily.

3.   Answer the following questions:

(a) In line 1, what is the case of *vincula*?
(b) In line 2, what part of its verb is *iacere*? Mention and translate all other examples of this part in the passage.
(c) In line 2, put *iussit* into the pluperfect.
(d) In line 4, what is the case of *Solō*?
(e) In line 5, what is the case of *Solō*?
(f) In line 6, put *dīxit* into the future.
(g) In line 6, what is the case of *Cȳrō*?
(h) In line 9, what part of which verb is *habēbat*?

The future of sum

Think of a verb which we've rather neglected for quite a long time, and it's a pretty important one too. Yes, you've got it. It's *sum*, and we must now go back to it, to learn its future.

1st person singular	*erō*	I shall be
2nd person singular	*eris*	you (sing.) will be
3rd person singular	*erit*	he, she, it will be
1st person plural	*erimus*	we shall be
2nd person plural	*eritis*	you (plur.) will be
3rd person plural	*erunt*	they will be

Perhaps the best way to remember this is to think of it rhyming with our old friends *amābō, amābis, amābit* etc.

Exercise 4.10

Translate into English:

1. *haec mulier fessa erit.*
2. *hic puer vir nōtissimus erit.*
3. *hī mīlitēs ducī cārī erunt.*
4. *cēterī hominēs īratī erunt.*
5. *puellae perterritae erunt.*
6. *erisne laetissimus puerōrum?*
7. *dominī saevī nōn erunt.*
8. *crās in agrō nōn eritis.*
9. *quis amīcus meus erit?*
10. *mox in templō mēcum eris.*

Here's a nice little thought: *dūcis* = 'you (sing.) are leading', while *dŭcis* means 'of a leader'. Similarly *dūcēs* = 'you (sing.) will lead' while *dŭcēs* = 'leaders' (nom. and acc.). Oh! these quantities!

Exercise 4.11

Translate into Latin:

1. Who will be terrified?
2. This river will be very deep.
3. We shall be very angry.
4. You (plur.) will be in the town tomorrow.
5. Will you (sing.) be with us in the temple?
6. The soldiers' wounds will not be big.
7. Those old men will be tired.
8. These girls will be beautiful women.
9. I shall soon be in the island.
10. The rest of the soldiers will be safe.

As for the pluperfect of *sum* it is formed regularly from the perfect, *fuī*, i.e. it is *fueram,* and it is regular all through. Mercifully, pluperfects are distinctly unenterprising. Let us remember while we are at it that the infinitive of *sum* is *esse*; the imperative (2nd person singular) is *es*, the plural is *este*. We shall very soon be returning to *sum* in a more exciting context.

cīvis

For the moment, however, there is plenty of excitement right here. You may have thought that we had shot our bolt as far as 3rd declension nouns are concerned; but this is far from true. In fact, we have a lot still to come. So here's a new type of 3rd declension noun:

cīvis, cīvis, c. = 'a citizen'		
	Singular	**Plural**
Nominative	*cīvis*	*cīvēs*
Vocative	*cīvis*	*cīvēs*
Accusative	*cīvem*	*cīvēs*
Genitive	*cīvis*	*cīvium*
Dative	*cīvī*	*cīvibus*
Ablative	*cīve*	*cīvibus*

The difference between *cīvis* and *rēx* is that the genitive plural of *rēx* is *regum* while that of *cīvis* is *cīvium*.

There is a general rule that a noun which increases in the genitive singular, forms its genitive plural in '*um*', while a noun that does not increase in its genitive singular, forms its genitive plural in '*ium*'.

Thus *rēx*, with one syllable, has two syllables in the genitive singular: *rēgis*. It has therefore increased, and its genitive plural is *rēgum*. But *cīvis*, with two syllables, still has only two syllables in its genitive singular: *cīvis*. It has therefore not increased, and its genitive plural is *cīvium*.

That's all very nice, but unfortunately, even in our selection of 3rd declension nouns, there are quite a lot of exceptions to this rule.

We have already met *pater, māter* and *frāter;* these 'family' nouns do not increase in the genitive singular, yet their genitives plural are *patrum, mātrum,* and *frātrum.* Similarly the genitive plural of *iuvenis* is *iuvenum*, and of *senex* is *senum,* although these too do not increase in the genitive singular.

Oh, and just to keep us guessing, both forms *parentum* and *parentium* are found in the genitive plural of *parēns, parentis,* m./f. = 'a parent'; though *parentium* is said to be more common.

However, stick to the rule unless we tell you it is broken. Thus we can happily give the genitive plural of *mīles, mīlitis* as *mīlitum* and that of *nāvis, nāvis* (see below) as *nāvium*.

Like *cīvis* go:
nāvis, nāvis, f. = 'ship'
hostis, hostis, c. = 'enemy'

hostis means an enemy of your country, not your personal enemy. It is nearly always masculine, and it is nearly always used in the plural: *hostēs, -ium.* Note that when we say 'the enemy' we mean a whole lot of enemies; in other words, though 'the enemy' in English is grammatically singular, it is plural in sense, and should be translated into the plural in Latin. If it is the subject of the sentence, the verb should be plural.

3rd declension monosyllables

Finally, here are four more nouns:

mōns, montis, m. = mountain
mors, mortis, f. = death
pars, partis, f. = part
urbs, urbis, f. = city

These go by a rule of their own, which takes precedence over the rule of increasing or not. This new rule applies to monosyllables whose stems end in two consonants. Such nouns form their genitives plural in *'-ium'*. Thus, the genitive plural of *mōns,* whose stem is *mont-,* is *montium;* and the genitives plural of *mors, pars* and *urbs* are *mortium, partium* and *urbium.*

You will, of course, meet 3rd declension monosyllables whose stem does *not* end in two consonants, such as *dux, ducis* (stem: *duc-*). Such nouns go *-um* in the genitive plural.

What a lot of lovely rules! And rules within rules! Rules! Where would we be without them?

Exercise 4.12

Give the genitive singular and genitive plural of:

1.	*hostis*	6.	*pars*
2.	*rēx*	7.	*dux*
3.	*urbs*	8.	*māter*
4.	*mōns*	9.	*pater*
5.	*mīles*	10.	*mulier*

Exercise 4.13

Translate into English:

1.	*Rōmānī hostēs vīcērunt.*	6.	*haec pars urbis pulchrior est quam illa.*
2.	*rēx ducēs cīvium nōn amābat.*	7.	*illa puella parentibus cārissima est.*
3.	*estne Rōma urbium pulcherrima?*	8.	*quid dē morte dīxit Solō?*
4.	*hic mōns montium altissimus est.*	9.	*bellum nōbīscum hostēs gerent.*
5.	*hostium mīlitēs multī erant.*	10.	*hī virī nāvium ducēs sunt*

Exercise 4.14

Translate into Latin:

1.	The inhabitants will hurry into the new city.	6.	Will this boy fear the anger of the citizens?
2.	That part of the mountains is the highest.	7.	Those farmers' bodies are very strong.
3.	The enemy will soon attack the town.	8.	The leaders of the enemy are very famous.
4.	These soldiers do not fear death.	9.	This youth is a friend of my brothers'.
5.	Where are the old men's swords?	10.	Is Rome the most famous of cities?

Exercise 4.15

Link up the following Latin words (1-6) with the English ones (a-f). Explain the connexion between the English words and the Latin words from which they are derived.

1.	*cīvis*	(a)	urban
2.	*mōns*	(b)	hostile
3.	*mors*	(c)	mortal
4.	*nāvis*	(d)	civilian
5.	*urbs*	(e)	mountain
6.	*hostēs*	(f)	naval

Exercise 4.16

Read the following passage carefully, and answer the questions on it.

The Story of Narcissus: Part 1

1 *fuit iuvenis, nōmine Narcissus; pulcherrimus ille iuvenum erat; multae illum puellae et multī puerī amīcum habēre cupīvērunt; sed ille hōrum <u>nēminem</u> habēre cupīvit amīcum; <u>nēminem</u> laudāvit; cum puerīs et puellīs*
5 *numquam lūsit. ōlim ille, ubi in <u>silvā</u> fuit sōlus, <u>fontem lūcidissimum</u> vīdit et, quod bibere cōnstituit, <u>fontī appropinquāvit</u>; et, ubi aquam spectāvit, <u>ōs</u> ibi vīdit pulcherrimī iuvenis et statim amīcus esse illīus iuvenis magnopere cupīvit; et illum bracchiīs salūtāvit, et ille*
10 *Narcissum salūtāvit; et dīxit Narcissus iuvenī 'ego Narcissus sum; quis es tū?' iuvenis tamen nōn respondit.*

nēminem is the accusative of
  nēmō (irregular) = no one
silva, -ae, f. = wood, forest
fōns, fontis, m. (here)
  = spring
lūcidus, -a, -um = clear
appropinquō, -āre, -āvī, -ātum
  (+ dat.) = I approach
ōs, ōris, n. (here) = face
bracchium, -i, n. = arm

1. Answer the following questions:

    (a) In lines 1-3, why do you think the boys and girls wanted Narcissus as a friend?
    (b) In lines 3-5, describe Narcissus' attitude to the boys and girls.
    (c) In line 5, does the word *sōlus* surprise you here? Explain your answer.
    (d) In line 6, why is it significant that the spring is described as *lūcidissimum*?
    (e) In lines 6-7, why did Narcissus approach the spring?
    (f) In lines 7-8, we read *ōs ibi vīdit pulcherrimī iuvenis.* Is this literally true? Explain yet again!
    (g) In lines 8-9, how was Narcissus affected by what he saw in the water?
    (h) In line 9, can you think of a neat translation for *illum bracchiīs salūtāvit*?

2. Translate the passage beautifully.

3. Answer the following questions:

    (a) In line 1, what case of what noun is *nōmine*? Translate it.
    (b) In line 1, comment on the form *iuvenum* – in full.
    (c) In line 3, put *cupīvērunt* into the imperfect.
    (d) In line 4, we read *cum puerīs et puellīs*; if we had wanted to say 'with the boy and the girl' what would we have written?
    (e) *lūsit* (line 5); what are the principal parts of this verb?
    (f) In line 7, put *vīdit* into the pluperfect.
    (g) In line 9, put *illum* and *ille* into the neuter.
    (h) In line 10 we have the word *ego* (= I); how would you say 'with me' in Latin?

Exercise 4.17

Translate into Latin:

1. The women were warning the bad inhabitants.
2. The angry teachers do not praise the tired boys.
3. The queen is calling the little maid-servants.
4. The savage master frightens the slave.
5. The farmers were moving the shields.
6. They will not defeat the Romans.
7. Will the savage soldiers attack our city?
8. Who will come to the temple with us?
9. The old men will be in the fields tomorrow.
10. We shall soon be on those ships.

possum

Remember my promise to bring in our old friend *sum* very soon again? I'm also sure that you remember how we added *ad* or *ab* to *sum*, producing *adsum* = 'I am present' and *absum* = 'I am absent'. Well, here's something similar.

Long ago there was an old adjective called *potis* (or sometimes *pote*). We shall be saying a lot about this type of adjective pretty soon. Now *potis*, or *pote*, meant 'able' and, if we add this to *sum* we get 'I am able' or 'I can'. And this is how we should add them: before a part of *sum* starting with 's', such as *sum* itself, we add *pos-*, while before a part of *sum* starting with 'e' we add *pot-*. It's as easy as that, all the way through. So, as long as you know *sum*, you know *possum*.

possum, posse, potuī = 'I can', 'am able'

Present

1st person singular	possum	I can, am able
2nd person singular	potes	you (sing.) can, are able
3rd person singular	potest	he, she, it can, is able
1st person plural	possumus	we can, are able
2nd person plural	potestis	you (plur.) can, are able
3rd person plural	possunt	they can, are able

Future

1st person singular	poterō	I shall be able
2nd person singular	poteris	you (sing.) will be able
3rd person singular	poterit	he, she, it will be able
1st person plural	poterimus	we shall be able
2nd person plural	poteritis	you (plur.) will be able
3rd person plural	poterunt	they will be able

Imperfect

1st person singular	poteram	I was able
2nd person singular	poterās	you (sing.) were able
3rd person singular	poterat	he, she, it was able
1st person plural	poterāmus	we were able
2nd person plural	poterātis	you (plur.) were able
3rd person plural	poterant	they were able

The present infinitive, admittedly, presents us with a tiny little hiccough; it is *posse* = 'to be able'. The perfect is pathetically easy: it is *potuī*, regular throughout; and the pluperfect, *potueram*, is quite shamefully regular too. Finally, *possum* has no imperative.

So, there's *possum* for you. The secret of *possum*, once you've got the idea, is to say its different tenses to yourself over and over again, always remembering that it is a compound of *sum*.

Exercise 4.18

Give the Latin for:

1. He can sing.
2. You (sing.) can write.
3. She cannot read.
4. We cannot see.
5. You (pl.) can run.
6. They can sail.
7. I was not able to fight.
8. We were not able to read.
9. They were not able to sleep.
10. Can you (pl.) hear?
11. I shall be able to fight.
12. He had been able to sing.
13. To be able to see.
14. She has not been able to come.
15. We were not able to work.
16. Will you (sing.) be able to come?
17. You (pl.) have been able to sleep.
18. You (sing.) had been able to rule.
19. I cannot see you, Laelia.
20. You (pl.) were not able to see me.

Exercise 4.19

Translate into English:

1. *hī puerī in templō cantāre nōn possunt.*
2. *quis potest agrōs ex oppidō vidēre?*
3. *mox per hoc flūmen nāvigāre poterō.*
4. *poteruntne hostēs Rōmānōs superāre?*
5. *hae puellae ex oppidō ad mare currere poterant.*
6. *poterimusne diū in agrīs labōrāre?*
7. *senex sum; festīnāre nōn possum.*
8. *haec mulier cibum bene parāre potest.*
9. *librum scrībere nōn potuī.*
10. *illī ducēs hostēs vincere nōn potuērunt.*

Exercise 4.20

Translate into Latin:

1. Can you (pl.) see the enemy's soldiers?
2. I cannot read this book.
3. She wants to be able to sing in the temple.
4. They will be able to sail to the island.
5. We have been able to overcome the enemy.
6. Who was able to build this wall?
7. They can work for a long time.
8. He is able to run to the city.
9. They have been able to stay in the town.
10. Are you (pl.) able to fight with the enemy?

Note that in English *poteram* (imperfect) and *potuī* (past) can both be translated as 'I was able'.

Incidentally, 'I could' is a very tricky customer. It can be a past tense, e.g. 'When I was tested yesterday, I could do it easily'; or it can refer to the future, e.g. 'If I had to do this next week, I could do it easily'. Better give 'could' a wide berth!

Vocabulary 4

Vocabulary 4

cīvis, cīvis, c. = citizen
nāvis, nāvis, f. = ship
hostēs, hostium, c. pl. = the enemy
hic, haec, hoc = this
ille, illa, illud = that
corpus, corporis, n. = body
vulnus, vulneris, n. = wound

cēterī, -ae, -a = the rest (of)
paucī, -ae, -a = few, a few
frūstrā = in vain
quoque = also, too
appropinquō, -āre, -āvī, -ātum (+ dat.) = I approach
cōnspiciō, -ere, -spexī, -spectum = I catch sight of
līberō, -āre, -āvī, -ātum = I set free

N.B.   *quoque* is always written after its word, e.g. *māter quoque* = 'the mother also.'

So here we are consuming chapter after chapter greedily in our usual way. Still, there's more than half left. (I've always been rather good, if you'll excuse my modesty, at mental arithmetic.)

Chapter 5

nōnne and num

It's about time we started to ask some more questions; and this time we're especially interested in answers.

You can distinguish very clearly in Latin between a question that expects the answer 'yes' and one that expects the answer 'no'. And the same is almost true of English.

For example, if we ask 'Isn't this Quintus' book?' we are implying that it is and that the person whom we are asking will say 'yes'. Such a question in Latin would be introduced by *nōnne*.

e.g.   *nōnne hic Quīntī liber est?*

A close look at *nōnne* will tell us that the '*-ne*' shows that it is asking a question, and the '*nōn*' means 'not'. So this is exactly the same as English.

If, on the other hand, we are expecting the answer 'no', we would introduce the question with *num*. For this we don't have such a definite word in English. Perhaps the best translation of *num hic Quīntī liber est?* would be 'Is this really Quintus' book?'

Exercise 5.1

Translate into English:

1.   *nōnne Rōmānī hostēs semper vincent?*
2.   *num illōrum patria pulchrior est nostrā?*
3.   *nōnne hostium mīlitēs oppidum illud oppugnābant?*
4.   *nōnne crās agricolae in agrīs labōrābunt?*
5.   *num herī in templō cantāvērunt?*
6.   *nōnne haec mulier pulcherrima est?*
7.   *num hic puer in urbem festīnābit?*
8.   *num bonum est gladiīs et hastīs pugnāre?*
9.   *nōnne in illō oppidō cibum cōnsūmet?*
10.   *num huius īnsulae incolae laetī sunt?*

Exercise 5.2

Translate into Latin:

1. Are those farmers really in the town?
2. Won't the teachers praise this boy?
3. Is this horse really your father's?
4. Haven't these soldiers fought with those?
5. Will he really run to the sea with me?
6. Isn't that woman hurrying to the temple?
7. Are those leaders really leading the ships?
8. Aren't the maid-servants preparing the food?
9. Did they really run down from the mountain?
10. Haven't those boys read this book?

Now for some quite different things.

postquam and antequam

These two words are both conjuctions introducing subordinate clauses: *postquam* = 'after'; *antequam* = 'before'. Both regularly start a sentence. Thus:

> *postquam per agrōs ambulāvī, in urbem vēnī* =
> 'After I had walked through the fields, I came into the city.'

> *antequam in urbem vēnī, per agrōs ambulāvī* =
> 'Before I came into the city, I walked through the fields.'

Notes:

(i) The Latin pluperfect is very rare after *postquam*. Although in English we often use a pluperfect ('had') after the word 'after', in Latin the perfect is used.

(ii) The word *antequam* is sometimes chopped in half as follows:

> *ante per agrōs ambulāvī, quam in urbem vēnī* =
> 'I walked through the fields before I came into the city.'

In this example *ante...quam* governs *vēnī* ('before I came...'), not *ambulāvī*.

We shall say more later about the dastardly dangers that lie hidden in the English words 'before' and 'after'. For the moment, suffice it to learn this little ditty and to recite it to yourself (day and night, of course) remembering that a clause must contain a verb.

> *antequam*, which means 'before'
> And *postquam* meaning 'after',
> Unless they introduce a clause
> Will earn derisive laughter.

Exercise 5.3

Translate into Latin:

1. After he had departed
2. After we had slept
3. After you (sing.) had heard
4. After I had run
5. After they had hurried
6. Before I arrived
7. Before you came
8. Before we attacked
9. Before they approached
10. Before you (pl.) saw

quamquam

Now, while we're on these subordinate clauses, here's an altogether new one. Excitement! These new clauses are called concessive clauses, because they concede or admit that, in spite of them, the main verb is true. These clauses are introduced in English by 'though' or 'although'. There are more than one word in Latin for 'though', but we shall confine ourselves to *quamquam,* which is a good honest word that will play no dirty tricks. It is quite affectionate and likes to be 'tucked in' (although this isn't compulsory). Remember our earlier subordinate clauses?

e.g.　*hostēs, quamquam fortiter pugnābant, Rōmānōs nōn superāvērunt =*
　　　'Although the enemy fought bravely, they did not overcome the Romans.'

Note that in English we do not, on the whole, go in for tucking in, and we have started the English sentence, not with 'the enemy', but with 'although'.

Exercise 5.4

Translate into English:

1.　*postquam discessērunt, librōs nostrōs lēgimus.*
2.　*antequam vēnērunt magistrī, puerī in templum cucurrērunt.*
3.　*senēs, quamquam fessī erant, in urbem festīnābant.*
4.　*postquam mūrum aedificāvērunt, laetī erant.*
5.　*nōn ante cibum parāvit quam cīvēs adfuērunt.*
6.　*mulierēs, quamquam vīnum bibēbant, miserae erant.*
7.　*postquam Quīntum, poētam, audīvit, illum magnopere laudāvit.*
8.　*ducem illum, quamquam mīlitēs bene dūxit, nōn laudāvimus.*
9.　*antequam vēnit dominus, ancillae perterritae erant.*
10.　*quamquam aderam, rēgem audīre nōn potuī.*

Exercise 5.5

Translate into Latin:

1.　Before the general entered the town, we feared him.
2.　Although the river was very long, it was not deep.
3.　After the poet had read his book, the citizens praised him.
4.　Before we came into the city, we were frightened.
5.　Although the teacher was angry, he did not utter[1] savage words.
6.　After the boys had sung in the temple, they departed through the fields.
7.　He approached the city before it was light.[2]
8.　Although I feared the citizens, I remained in the city.
9.　After they had sailed through the sea, they came to this island.
10.　Although these citizens are good, we do not love them.

[1] Use *dīcō.*
[2] Say 'there was light'.

And now for one or two nice little things before we continue the story of Narcissus.

Two new ways of saying 'and'

So far we have learnt from our earliest days, when we were metaphorically, as far as Latin went, in our swaddling-clothes, that the Latin for 'and' was *et*. However, you surely don't think the Romans left it at that! Here then are two new things you can play with:

(i)   *et...et* means 'both...and' and is extremely common.

e.g.   ***et** puerī **et** puellae* = '**both** the boys **and** the girls.'

Incidentally this may be a good place to say a little more about the fact that if we want to apply an adjective to both masculine and feminine nouns alike, i.e. if we want to say 'both the boys and the girls are good', we use the masculine plural alone. I'm sorry about this. However, to cover up this unfortunate fact, we should always put the masculine part of the nouns we are describing nearer than the feminine to the erring adjective.

e.g.   *et puellae et puerī bonī sunt* = 'Both the girls and the boys are good.'

(ii)   The second new way of saying 'and' is to use *-que*. This isn't quite so straightforward. Remember we could add *'-ne'* to a word when asking a neutral question (i.e. expecting no particular answer)? Well, this is something similar. *'-que'* meaning 'and' does not exist by itself, but only when tagged on to another word: thus *mātrēs patrē**sque*** = 'mothers **and** fathers.'

'-que' can be added to anything, except that it is rare after a short *'e'*; in other words you wouldn't add it on to *mare*. When joining together two clauses, *'-que'* is regularly written after the first word of the new clause.

e.g.   *hostium mīlitēs cum nostrīs pugnāvērunt, nostrī**que** mīlitēs tandem illōs vīcērunt* = 'The enemy's soldiers fought with ours, **and** our soldiers finally defeated them.'

The new clause starts with *nostrī* and so *'-que'* is tagged on to it. But we could equally well have written:

     hostium mīlitēs cum nostrīs pugnāvērunt, mīlitēsque nostrī tandem illōs vīcērunt.

In this case we have chosen to start the new clause with *mīlitēs*. We could also have said *'tandemque...'* or *'illōsque...'* or *'vīcēruntque...'* You want to look out for this, particularly when translating from Latin, always remembering that the word *before* *'-que'* must belong to the clause that follows. (By the way, the word before *'-que'* is often slightly stressed.)

Asyndeton

We've already had examples of this omission of a word for 'and' as follows: *mātrēs, patrēs, sorōrēs, frātrēs*. In English we would probably say 'mothers, fathers, sisters *and* brothers', but we should not do this in Latin: either we should have asyndeton as above or we should say *patrēs **et** mātrēs **et** sorōrēs **et** frātrēs,* having an 'and' each time.

Exercise 5.6

Translate into English:

1. *in oppidum vēnērunt et nautae et agricolae.*
2. *puerī, puellae, virī, mulierēs in templō cantābant.*
3. *cum hostibus pugnāre constituērunt cupīvēruntque.*
4. *ubi sunt nautae, agricolae, mīlitēs?*
5. *bonōs ducēs mīlitum nautārumque habēmus.*
6. *magister et puellās et puerōs laudābit.*
7. *per oppida perque agrōs festīnāvimus.*
8. *illae puellae bonae sunt pulchraeque.*
9. *et nōs et vōs mox in oppidō vidēbunt.*
10. *puerī aquam portant cibumque parant puellae.*

Exercise 5.7

Translate into Latin:

1. Both boys and girls play in these fields.
2. The mother greatly loves her sons and daughters.
3. The old men and the women are tired.
4. Those leaders were wicked and savage.
5. The teachers praised the boys and gave them presents.
6. I shall both walk and run to the temple.
7. We ate food and drank wine.
8. She is a most beautiful and happy woman.
9. They hurried through the fields and approached the city.
10. The sailors will sail through these rivers and through those seas.

Exercise 5.8

Read the passage below carefully, and answer the questions on it.

The Story of Narcissus: Part 2

1   *Narcissus igitur <u>dextram</u> suam iuvenī dabat, sed, ubi*
    haec aquam <u>tetigit</u>, iuvenis ille <u>nōn iam</u> ibi <u>appāruit</u>. tum
    Narcissus <u>dextram</u> <u>retrāxit</u>, et mox iterum iuvenem vīdit;
    et diū illum spectābat; et ille diū Narcissum spectābat;
5   *et <u>rīsit</u> Narcissus iuvenī; et <u>rīsit</u> ille Narcissō; sed*
    numquam illum Narcissus <u>tangere</u> potuit, numquam
    iuvenis Narcissō respondit; et Narcissus miserrimus erat.
    <u>nihil</u> cōnsūmere cupīvit, <u>nihil</u> bibere; sed semper aquam
    frūstrā spectat et tandem mortuus est. ubi tamen
10   *sorōrēs illīus frātrem <u>sepelīre</u> cōnstituunt, corpus*
    Narcissī <u>nōn iam</u> adest, sed in locō illīus <u>flōs</u> <u>appāruit</u>
    pulcherrimus; hunc <u>flōrem</u> etiam hodiē in <u>hortīs</u> nostrīs
    habēmus et hunc vocāmus narcissum.

dextra, -ae, f. = right hand
tangō, -ere, tetigī, tāctum = I touch
nōn iam = no longer
appāreō, -ēre, appāruī,
    appāritum = I am visible,
    appear
retrahō, -ere, -trāxī, -tractum =
    I draw back (trans.)
rīdeō, -ēre, rīsī, rīsum (here) =
    I smile at (+ dat.)
nihil = nothing
sepeliō, -īre, -īvī, sepultum = I bury
flōs, flōris, m. = flower
hortus, -ī, m. = a garden

1. Answer the following questions:

    (a) In lines 1-2, what caused the 'youth' to disappear?
    (b) In lines 2-3, how did Narcissus come to see the 'youth' again?
    (c) In lines 5-6 give one reason for Narcissus' unhappiness.
    (d) In lines 6-7 give another reason for Narcissus' unhappiness.
    (e) In line 8, mention a twofold symptom of Narcissus' misery.
    (f) In lines 9-12, were Narcissus' sisters able to bury him? Explain your answer.
    (g) In lines 11-13, what is a narcissus?
    (h) Could it be agreed that Narcissus deserved his fate? Explain in full.

2. Translate the passage flowerily.

3. Answer the following questions:

    (a) In line 2, what does *haec* stand for?
    (b) In line 4, put *spectābat* into the pluperfect.
    (c) In line 6, if, instead of 'Narcissus was able', we wanted to say 'Narcissus is able…', what should we write instead of *potuit*?
    (d) *respondit* (line 7): Give the principal parts of this verb.
    (e) Mention and translate all the infinitives in this passage.
    (f) *frātrem* (line 10): what is the genitive plural of this noun?
    (g) In line 10, what is the accusative singular of *corpus*?
    (h) *pulcherrimus* (line 12): what is the comparative of this word? Give the nominative singular, masculine, feminine and neuter of this form.

Compound verbs

The verb *recipiō* is a compound of *capiō*. We have already met compounds of *sum* such as *adsum* and *possum*. A compound consists of a simple verb preceded by a prefix. The prefix is frequently a preposition such as we met in *adsum*. Though *'re'* is not in itself a word, as a prefix it generally means 'back'. Thus we get 'I take back'. But why *recipiō*? This is quite a valuable little piece of knowledge, so listen carefully.

Nearly all verbs with *'a'* in their first syllable regularly change this *'a'* into an *'i'* in compounds. Thus we get *percipiō* from *per + capiō,* and the supine *captum* changes its *'a'* into an *'e'*, thus becoming *perceptum.* Knowing this, we have a good chance of working out the meaning of many a compound verb. Take for example *perficiō:* this is *per + faciō*, and its supine, from which we regularly get our English word, is *perfectum.* If we do something right through, the result will be *perfect.* Pretty good, eh?

More prepositions

Here again is something we haven't had for ages. In fact, you might well have thought that we had finished with these words once and for all. But no. Here are a lot of new prepositions for us to revel in. They are all followed by the accusative.

ante (+ acc.) = before (of time); in front of (of place).
circum (+ acc.) = around
inter (+ acc.) = among, between
post (+ acc.) = after (of time); behind (of place)
propter (+ acc.) = because of
super (+ acc.) = above

Exercise 5.9

Translate into English:

1.	*circum īnsulam*	6.	*ante bellum*
2.	*propter verba*	7.	*post proelia*
3.	*inter cīvēs*	8.	*propter īram*
4.	*post bellum*	9.	*post mūrōs*
5.	*super terram*	10.	*inter puellam et puerum*

Exercise 5.10

Translate into Latin:

1.	Around the walls	6.	Above the river
2.	Before the war	7.	Before the night
3.	In front of the temple	8.	After the night
4.	Around the islands	9.	Among the citizens
5.	Because of the mountains	10.	Between those brothers

Before and after

'Before' and 'after' are very tricky in English.

(i)   We have recently learnt that they can be followed by a clause, in which case they are translated by *antequam* or *postquam*.

e.g.   *postquam mātrem salūtāvit, discessit* = 'After he had greeted his mother, he departed.'

(ii)   When followed by a noun, they are prepositions.

e.g.   *post bellum, patrem salūtāvit* = 'He greeted his father after the war.'

(iii)   They can also be adverbs.

e.g.   *mātrem salūtāvit; posteā discessit* = 'He greeted his mother; after, he departed.'

This brings me to the rather silly piece about the chieftain whose head had just been chopped off:

'He walked and talked after his head was cut off.' Correctly punctuated, this would make slightly more sense:

'He walked and talked; after, his head was cut off.'

Exercise 5.11

Translate into English:

1.   *circum īnsulam mare saevum est.*
2.   *cīvēs, propter verba nūntiōrum, laetissimī erunt.*
3.   *et malī et bonī hominēs inter cīvēs urbis sunt.*
4.   *post illum rēgem, quis rēxit?*
5.   *super terram caelum clārissimum est.*
6.   *ante bellum, incolae laetī erant.*
7.   *post illa proelia, mīlitēs discessērunt.*
8.   *novum dominum, propter īram illīus, ancillae nōn amant.*
9.   *haec inter mulierēs pulcherrima est.*
10.   *inter rēgem et rēgīnam stetit parvus puer.*

Exercise 5.12

Translate into Latin:

1. Many boys are standing around the temple.
2. Who does not praise Quintus because of his books?
3. Among these citizens, many are my friends.
4. Many people are most unhappy because of the war.
5. Above our city are many mountains.
6. Who will rule our land after our king?
7. Who* inhabited this island before these inhabitants?
8. Between the first and second boy stands a girl.
9. There are many fields around the town.
10. He came after this boy but before that one.

*The plural of *quis* is *quī*

nēmō

The word *nēmō* means 'no one'. It is generally masculine, but can be feminine. It is a very odd customer indeed, since it has a totally normal type of 3rd declension accusative and dative, but no genitive or ablative. It goes thus:

nēmō, m./f. = 'no one'

Nominative	*nēmō*
Accusative	*nēminem*
Genitive	–
Dative	*nēminī*
Ablative	–

There is a way of getting round this lack of a genitive and ablative, which I shall mention once and not again. There is an adjective *nūllus* which means 'no', as in 'no paper', 'no pens', etc. It goes like *sōlus* (see page 33) and its genitive *nūllīus* is used as the genitive of *nēmō*, i.e. 'of no person'. Similarly its ablative *nūllō, nūllā, nūllō* acts as the ablative of *nēmō*. So there it is.

nihil

One more word remains for the moment; and this one, at last, really is easy: it is *nihil* and it means 'nothing'. It is only used in the nominative and accusative, which are the same, since it is neuter. We get our word 'nil' from the contracted form, *nīl*, so that's jolly.

Exercise 5.13

Translate into English:

1. *dux nēminem pūnīvit.*
2. *malus dominus servīs suīs nihil dabat.*
3. *inter hōs mīlitēs, nēmō saevus est.*
4. *in agrō nēminem vīdī.*
5. *ibi nihil bonum est.*
6. *illa scūta nēminī dabō.*
7. *in hōc librō nihil est.*
8. *hic senex nihil hodiē cōnsūmpsit.*

Exercise 5.14

Translate into Latin:

1. I saw no one in the city.
2. There is nothing here.
3. This soldier alone carried nothing out of the city.
4. Give no one a book, Marcus!
5. I fear no one.
6. The wicked king fears nothing.
7. No one wants to seize the town.
8. They will find nothing in the city.

Exercise 5.15

Mention an English word which the following Latin ones remind you of. Explain the connexion between the words you have chosen and the Latin ones from which they are derived.

1. *dōnum*
2. *frūstrā*
3. *possum*
4. *nihil**
5. *super*

*Try an English compound of this word.

Exercise 5.16

Translate into Latin:

1. The boys were holding beautiful books.
2. The savage sailors were attacking the town.
3. Good teachers praise good girls.
4. Wretched women were warning bad men.
5. The strong horse does not fear the big farmer.
6. Does this man really fear little girls?
7. Although he is a bad leader, he fights well.
8. After I had sailed to the island, I was tired.
9. They will run round the temple.
10. No one is giving gifts to these boys.

Exercise 5.17

Read the following passage carefully and answer the questions on it.

War: Romans v Romans

1 *Rōmānī ōlim cum Rōmānīs pugnābant; erat <u>ubīque</u> bellum*	*ubīque* = everywhere
saevissimum; magnī ducēs magnōs ducēs superābant.	*expello, -ere, expulī, expulsum*
multī cīvēs multōs cīvēs et vulnerābant et necābant;	= I drive out
multōs agricolās mīlitēs ex agrīs illōrum <u>expellēbant</u> et	*ipsī* = themselves
5 *agrōs illōs <u>ipsī</u> capiēbant. <u>ubīque</u> mors et <u>miseria</u> erant*	*miseria, -ae,* f. = wretchedness,
multōsque per <u>annōs</u> <u>rēgnābant</u>; et postquam ducēs	misery
vīcērunt ducēs, <u>restābat</u> ūnus, <u>C.</u> Iūlius Caesar: dē illō	*annus, -ī,* m. = year
multī dīcēbant 'Iūlius Caesar rēx noster esse cupit.'	*rēgnō, -āre, -āvī, -ātum =*
Rōmānī multōs per <u>annōs</u> rēgēs nōn habuerant; illōs nōn	I reign, hold sway
10 *amābant.*	*restō, -āre, restitī* = I remain
	C. = Gaius (see note on p. 76)

1. Answer the following questions:

   (a) In line 1, what kind of war is being referred to here?
   (b) In lines 2-3, describe the war.
   (c) In lines 4-5, why did the soldiers drive the farmers out of their fields?
   (d) In line 6, which words tell us that this wretched state of affairs was going on for a long time?
   (e) In lines 6-7, explain the outcome of the battles between the various leaders.
   (f) In lines 7-8, what did many suspect about Julius Caesar?
   (g) In lines 9-10, what kind of ruler did the Romans definitely dislike?

2. Translate the passage belligerently.

3. Answer the following questions:

   (a) In line 2, what is the case of the first *ducēs*?
   (b) In line 2, what is the case of the second *ducēs*?
   (c) In line 2, put *superābant* into the pluperfect tense.
   (d) In line 3, put *necābant* into the future tense.
   (e) In line 6, what is the case of *annōs* and why?
   (f) *ūnus* (line 7): put this word into the genitive singular.
   (g) *cupit* (line 8): if instead of saying 'desires' I wanted to say 'desired', what should I write
       instead of *cupit*?

Vocabulary 5

Vocabulary 5	
ante + acc. = before, in front of	*cōpiae, -ārum,* f. pl. = military forces
circum + acc. = around	*mora, -ae,* f. = delay
inter + acc. = among, between	*mulier, mulieris,* f. = woman
post + acc. = after, behind	*uxor, uxōris,* f. = wife
propter + acc. = because of	*fugiō, fugere, fūgī, fugitum* = I flee
super + acc. = above	*gerō, -ere, gessī, gestum* = I carry on, do,
nam = for	wage (a war)

Half time! Need I say more? Answer in full.

Chapter 6

melior = better

Remember our piece in Chapter 3, saying that some important adjectives throw their weight about when it comes to their comparative and superlative forms, just to show how special they are? Well, now is the time to sort them out, starting with *melior*.

Positive	**Comparative**	**Superlative**
bonus	*melior*	*optimus*

The superlative declines like *bonus*; the comparative is 3rd declension and declines like *laetior* (see page 27).

melior, melius = 'better'

Singular

	Masculine	**Feminine**	**Neuter**
Nominative	*melior*	*melior*	*melius*
Vocative	*melior*	*melior*	*melius*
Accusative	*meliōrem*	*meliōrem*	*melius*
Genitive	*meliōris*	*meliōris*	*meliōris*
Dative	*meliōrī*	*meliōrī*	*meliōrī*
Ablative	*meliōre*	*meliōre*	*meliōre*

Plural

Nominative	*meliōrēs*	*meliōrēs*	*meliōra*
Vocative	*meliōrēs*	*meliōrēs*	*meliōra*
Accusative	*meliōrēs*	*meliōrēs*	*meliōra*
Genitive	*meliōrum*	*meliōrum*	*meliōrum*
Dative	*meliōribus*	*meliōribus*	*meliōribus*
Ablative	*meliōribus*	*meliōribus*	*meliōribus*

Incidentally, this may remind you of the French '*meilleur*'. Or there again, it may not.

Exercise 6.1

Translate into English:

1. *hī librī meliōrēs sunt illīs.*
2. *magna scūta meliōra sunt quam parva.*
3. *laetus dominus melior est quam miser.*
4. *nostrī mīlitēs meliōrēs sunt vestrīs.*
5. *dā hunc librum meliōrī puerō.*
6. *magister meliōrēs puellās laudāvit.*
7. *quis cum meliōribus comitibus ambulāre cupit?*
8. *haec meliōrum puellārum prīma est.*

Exercise 6.2

Rewrite the first four sentences of Exercise 6.1, giving a version for 'than' different from the one used.

e.g.   '*hic puer melior est illō*' would become '*hic puer melior est quam ille.*'

e.g.   '*hae urbēs meliōrēs sunt quam illae*' would become '*hae urbēs illīs meliōrēs sunt.*'

Exercise 6.3

Translate into Latin:

1.   Who is better than Caesar?
2.   These beautiful rivers are better than those.
3.   Is there not a better road than this?
4.   The better horses were standing in the better field.
5.   These are the books of the better old man.
6.   The strong youths are better than the wicked ones.
7.   The farmers are better than the sailors.
8.   Are these really the better towns?
9.   Good leaders are better than a bad king.
10.   A good king is better than bad leaders.

optimus = best

So much for 'better'. Now for the superlative of *bonus*, which is *optimus* (= 'best' or 'very good').
Here we have a word which is not only totally unlike *bonus*, but is also rather splendidly, I must admit,
unlike *melior* too. It has the decency, however, to decline like *bonus*, so that's one thing.

Exercise 6.4

Translate into English:

1.   *estne hic optimus puerōrum?*
2.   *estne hīc optimus puerōrum?*
3.   *in hōc oppidō optimum templum est.*
4.   *illī hominēs in optimā parte urbis habitant.*
5.   *optimōs agricolās in hōc agrō vīdī.*
6.   *hī virī optima templa laudant.*
7.   *magister pulchrum librum optimae puellae dedit.*
8.   *dominus optimōs servōs statim vidēre cupit.*
9.   *nūntiī īrātī mīlitēs optimōs nōn laudāvērunt.*
10.   *vestrī parentēs vōbīs optimum magistrum lēgērunt.*

Exercise 6.5

Translate into Latin:

1.   The queen loves the best maid-servant.
2.   Is this the best of the rivers?
3.   That boy is the best.
4.   The poet sang to the very good girl.
5.   Oh! best of kings. We shall praise you.
6.   You (pl.) will walk to the town with the very good soldiers.
7.   He is the teacher of the best girls.
8.   The very good citizens hear very good words.

peior = worse

So much for 'better' and 'best', but alas, we can't always stay on this lofty plane; let us briefly, but painfully, descend to 'worse' and even 'worst'. The word *malus* would not be content with giving us a straightforward comparative. Instead, the Latin for 'worse' is *peior* and it goes as follows:

Singular	**Masculine**	**Feminine**	**Neuter**
Nominative	*peior*	*peior*	*peius*
Vocative	*peior*	*peior*	*peius*
Accusative	*peiōrem*	*peiōrem*	*peius*
Genitive	*peiōris*	*peiōris*	*peiōris*
Dative	*peiōrī*	*peiōrī*	*peiōrī*
Ablative	*peiōre*	*peiōre*	*peiōre*
Plural			
Nominative	*peiōrēs*	*peiōrēs*	*peiōra*
Vocative	*peiōrēs*	*peiōrēs*	*peiōra*
Accusative	*peiōrēs*	*peiōrēs*	*peiōra*
Genitive	*peiōrum*	*peiōrum*	*peiōrum*
Dative	*peiōribus*	*peiōribus*	*peiōribus*
Ablative	*peiōribus*	*peiōribus*	*peiōribus*

For the pronunciation of *peior,* see note on page 22 on *huius.* Note that *peior* differs from regular comparatives in that we only add *-or* to the stem (not *-ior*).

Exercise 6.6

Translate into English:

1. *hae undae peiōrēs sunt illīs.*
2. *malus iuvenis peior est quam malus senex.*
3. *'quid est malō ventō peius?' dīcit nauta.*
4. *illī nautae peiōra verba dīcēbant.*
5. *illa oppida hīs peiōra sunt.*
6. *servī dominōrum rēgis servīs peiōrēs sunt.*
7. *peiōrēs puerōs nōn amat magister.*
8. *illī agrī peiōrum agricolārum sunt.*

Exercise 6.7

Translate into Latin:

1. Those books are worse than these.
2. Who is worse than this wicked soldier?
3. Are savage winds worse than savage waves?
4. Tired generals are worse than bad (ones).
5. 'What is worse than a king?' said the Romans.
6. The teacher did not praise the worse boys.
7. These towns are worse than that city.
8. These are the books of the worse inhabitants.

pessimus = worst

The superlative of *malus* is *pessimus*. It means 'worst' or 'very bad' and is completely regular, going like *bonus*. (Notice how we have kindly introduced these horrors one by one.)

Exercise 6.8

Translate into English:

1. *hae ancillae pessimae sunt.*
2. *pessimī agricolae pessimōs agrōs habent.*
3. *rēgēs nōn semper pessimī sunt.*
4. *illōs hominēs, quod pessimī sunt, magnopere timeō.*
5. *num pessimam urbem hanc amās?*
6. *quis pessimōs laudat?*
7. *magister pessimās puellās nōn laudābit.*
8. *dominus pessimō servō pecūniam nōn dedit.*

Exercise 6.9

Translate into Latin:

1. This city is the worst.
2. Marcus gave this sword to the worst leader.
3. Who is the worst of these old men?
4. Those youths are very bad.
5. They live in the worst town.
6. What is the worst (thing) in this city?
7. The worst sailors will have very bad ships.
8. Oh! worst of soldiers, depart (pl.)!

is, ea, id

We shall soon return to comparatives and superlatives, but let us now for a moment turn our attention to an extremely important little word. Its importance is vastly greater than its size! It is *is* (= 'that') and is used to refer to someone or something that is further than *hic* but a little nearer than *ille*. The pronoun *is* is the commonest word for 'he, she, it' when the word in question is neither particularly near nor particularly far.

is, ea, id = 'that'; 'he', 'she', 'it'			
Singular	**Masculine**	**Feminine**	**Neuter**
Nominative	*is*	*ea*	*id*
Accusative	*eum*	*eam*	*id*
Genitive	*eius*	*eius*	*eius*
Dative	*eī*	*eī*	*eī*
Ablative	*eō*	*eā*	*eō*
Plural			
Nominative	*eī, iī*	*eae*	*ea*
Accusative	*eōs*	*eās*	*ea*
Genitive	*eōrum*	*eārum*	*eōrum*
Dative	*eīs, iīs*	*eīs, iīs*	*eīs, iīs*
Ablative	*eīs, iīs*	*eīs, iīs*	*eīs, iīs*

Notes:
(i)   The genitive *eius* is really '*eiius*'; the second '*i*' is no longer written, but the first syllable is
       long, since the '*e*' is still regarded as being followed by two consonantal '*i*'s. But the '*e*' is not
       long by nature and should **not** be pronounced long. See note on *huius*, page 22.

(ii)   *eī* (dat. sing. and nom. masc. pl.) consists of two distinct syllables (i.e. it is not a diphthong).

(iii) We shall not use the alternative forms *iī* and *iīs,* but we thought you ought to know them; in fact
       iī is thought to be commoner than *eī* in the nominative plural.

(iv)   Beware; in translating 'it' into Latin, we must use the gender of the Latin noun which 'it' stands
       for.

e.g.   'There is an island there; can't you see **it**'? = '*ibi est īnsula; nōnne **eam** vidēre potes?*'

Exercise 6.10

Translate into English:

1.   *ea mulier mea uxor est.*
2.   *quid id est? id scūtum est.*
3.   *hic liber eius puerī est; eum amat.*
4.   *servī bene labōrant; dominus igitur eōs laudābit.*
5.   *eās puellās in templum intrāre iubē.*
6.   *urbs ea pulchra est; eī appropinquābō.*
7.   *mīlitem hostēs eā sagittā vulnerāvērunt; eam dēlēbō.*
8.   *ea oppida hostēs oppugnant.*
9.   *ubi est Gnaeus? quis eum vīdit?*
10.   *Sulpicia Gnaeum vīdit; rogā eam.*

Exercise 6.11

Translate into Latin, using parts of *is* for 'that' and 'those', 'he', 'she', 'it' and 'they':

1.   Where are those women? I wish to see them.
2.   Do you see this man? This sword is his.
3.   Those slaves are very good; we shall therefore give them many gifts.
4.   Those boys are holding these books.
5.   The sailor is wicked; I shall order him to depart.
6.   The slaves are good; we shall therefore give them to good masters.
7.   We shall sail along these rivers.
8.   Were you happy because of those words, Marcus?
9.   There are many islands in this sea; but our sailors will sail around them.
10.   The boy has not worked well; therefore I shall not praise him.

Learning to 'understand'

It's time we returned now to Julius Caesar and all those people who feared that he was planning to
become king. But before we do, here's another little thing for you to put under your hat. You will
sometimes hear us saying that a word (or words) are 'understood'. To 'understand' is to treat a word (or
words) as being in a sentence when they are not actually there. We came across this when we learnt that
bonī could mean 'good men', even though the word for 'men' was not there. Look out for this in the
following exercise; it could prove useful.

Exercise 6.12

Read the following passage carefully and answer the questions on it.

War: Julius Caesar is removed

1   *Iūlius Caesar rēx nōn fuit; nam eum Brūtus cum*
    comitibus necāvit; multī tum laetī sed multī īrātī erant; et
    saeva proelia fuērunt inter illōs et hōs. Caesar <u>adoptāverat</u>
    et <u>hērēdem</u> fēcerat iuvenem, nōmine <u>Octāviānum</u>; is fīlius
5   *erat <u>Atiae</u>; ea fīlia erat Iūliae, et ea Iūlia soror erat Iūliī*
    Caesaris. ubi <u>Octāviānus</u> parvus puer erat, pater eius
    Octāvius <u>mortuus est</u> et, ubi Iūlium Caesarem Brūtus et
    comitēs eius necāvērunt, <u>ūndēvīgintī</u> <u>annōs nātus</u> erat.
    tum et māter eius Atia et novus coniūnx mātris,
10 *Philippus, <u>Octāviānum</u> sīc monēbant: 'tū iuvenis es; malī*
    virī tē superābunt et necābunt. manē hīc nōbīscum, et
    tūtus eris.' sed <u>Octāviānus</u> cum eīs nōn mānsit.

adoptō, -āre, -āvī, -ātum =
  I adopt
hērēs, hērēdis, c. = heir, heiress
Octāviānus, -ī, m. = Octavian
Atia, -ae, f. = Atia (mother of
  Octavian)
mortuus est = (he) died
ūndēvīgintī = nineteen
annōs nātus = years old

Note:
ūndēvīgintī (line 8) = 'nineteen' (one from twenty): being indeclinable, like *vīgintī* (= 'twenty') itself, it does not change, whatever its case.

1. Answer the following questions:

    (a) In lines 1-2, what prevented Caesar from being king?
    (b) In lines 2-3, describe the general situation after Caesar's death.
    (c) In lines 4-6, what was the exact blood relationship of Octavian to Caesar?
    (d) In lines 6-8, what happened to Octavian (i) when he was a small boy, and (ii) when he was
        19 years old?
    (e) In lines 9-10, what relation of Octavian's was Philippus?
    (f) In line 10, what point is being made by use of the word *iuvenis*?
    (g) In lines 11-12, what was Atia and Philippus' advice to Octavian?
    (h) In line 12, how did Octavian respond to it?

2. Translate the passage violently.

3. Answer the following questions:

    (a) In line 2, which case of which noun is *comitibus*?
    (b) In line 2, what do we 'understand' with each *multī*?
    (c) *fēcerat* (line 4): what is the tense and from which verb does this come?
    (d) *pater eius Octāvius* (lines 6-7): *Octāvius* is in ap.....ion to *pater.* Can you fill in the gap correctly?
    (e) *necāvērunt* (line 8): put this verb into the imperfect.
    (f) *monēbant* (line 10): if we wished to say 'they will warn', what would this word become?
    (g) In line 11, what part of which verb is *manē*? Give its principal parts and meaning.
    (h) In line 11, how can we be sure what *hīc* means here (no pun intended)? What does it not
        mean here?

The former and latter

In Latin we use *ille* and *hic* for 'the former' and 'the latter'. Because 'the former' is further away (in the sentence) than 'the latter', we use *ille* for 'the former'; and because 'the latter' is nearer, we use *hic*.

e.g.　*Aulus et Gnaeus puerī sunt; ille bonus, hic malus est.*
　　　Aulus and Gnaeus are boys; the former is good, the latter is bad.

Suus and eius

Suus is very rare in the nominative, because it is reflexive. It means 'his own', 'her own', 'its own' or 'their own'.

e.g.　*Mārcus amīcōs suōs amat =*
　　　'Marcus loves his own friends.'

　　　Mārcus et Laelia mātrem suam amant =
　　　'Marcus and Laelia love their mother.'

One way of dealing with *suus* is to say that it means 'belonging to the subject of the sentence'. If you want to say 'his' or 'her' (belonging to someone else), you must use *eius*.

e.g.　*Mārcus Gāium amat; amīcōs tamen eius nōn amat =*
　　　'Marcus loves Gaius; he does not, however, love his (i.e. Gaius') friends.'

The same goes for 'their'. If 'their' means 'their own', use *suus*; if it means belonging to some other people, use *eōrum* or *eārum*, according to the gender required. (You will see that English is terribly ambiguous most of the time.)

e.g.　*amīcōs suōs amant; nōn tamen amīcōs eōrum amant.*
　　　'They love their own friends; however they do not love *their* friends' (i.e. some other people's).

Now, then – here are some new verbs. We are in a generous mood, aren't we? You'd better make the best of it.

occupō, -āre, -āvī, -ātum = I seize (a place)
colligō, colligere, collēgī, collēctum = I collect
dēfendō, dēfendere, dēfendī, defēnsum = I defend
occīdō, occīdere, occīdī, occīsum = I kill
trādō, trādere, trādidī, trāditum = I hand over

Exercise 6.13

Translate into English:

1.　*Sulpicia Mārcum amat; sorōrēs tamen eius nōn amat.*
2.　*Sulpicia sorōrēs suās amat.*
3.　*Mārcus bonum amīcum habet; eius tamen patriam nōn dēfendet.*
4.　*hī puerī multōs amīcōs habent, et eōrum amīcōs amant.*
5.　*hae puellae suōs parentēs magnopere amant.*
6.　*Mārcus cum Gnaeō pugnat; ille hunc superābit.*
7.　*ubi Rōmānī cum hostibus bellum gerunt, illī hōs vincunt.*
8.　*cīvēs ex suā urbe fugiunt.*
9.　*ille urbem eōrum dēfendet.*
10.　*hī patriam suam dēfendēbant.*

Exercise 6.14

Translate into Latin, using *suus* for 'his/her/its/their (own)' and *eius, eōrum* or *eārum* elsewhere:

1. He handed over his own books to me.
2. Hand her books over to me, boy!
3. We took their swords.
4. The soldiers will collect their own spears.
5. Sulpicia and Laelia are here; the former is very happy and the latter is very beautiful.
6. Who will flee out of his own city?
7. The king rules his own citizens.
8. We are sailing along their river.
9. He loves these girls and their parents.
10. Marcus and Gaius are in the field; the latter is tired, the former is not.

Needless to say, if no gender is given (or understood) for 'their', we use the masculine form.

Exercise 6.15

Of what English words do the following Latin ones remind you? Explain the connexion between the Latin words and the English ones you have chosen.

1. *occupō*
2. *dēfendō*
3. *colligō*
4. *trādō*
5. *fugiō*
6. *optimus*
7. *pessimus*
8. *circum*

Exercise 6.16

Translate into Latin:

1. The big girls were watching the sky.
2. The good woman is carrying the food.
3. The masters were freeing the happy slaves.
4. Angry teachers do not praise bad boys.
5. The boys were entering the sacred river.
6. Strong soldiers are defending those tired old men.
7. These generals have seized his great city.
8. What is the teacher showing him?
9. The citizens were fleeing into their own city.
10. Show me your book, Laelia! I want to see it.

Exercise 6.17

Read the following passage carefully and answer the questions on it. This is so exciting that we are using the historic present throughout.

War: peace!

1   *Octāviānus <u>paulātim</u> <u>aliōs</u> ducēs superat; multōs ante occīdit quam illī eum occīdere possunt: tandem sōlī Antōnius et Cleopatra, <u>Aegyptī</u> rēgīna, <u>restant</u>; et illōs Agrippa, amīcus Octāviānī, prope Actium, oppidum*
5   *Graecum, in proeliō nāvium vincit. tum Octāviānus sōlus <u>cūnctōrum</u> <u>prīnceps</u> est; et <u>cūnctīs</u> <u>quī</u> cum eō pugnāvērunt <u>parcit</u>. <u>callidissimus</u> est et, quamquam <u>cūnctōs</u> regit, <u>urbānissimus</u> est. eum <u>nōn iam</u> Octāviānum vocant hominēs sed Augustum; is multōs*
10   *per <u>annōs</u> regit; et dōnum pulcherrimum dat Augustus hominibus: <u>pācem</u> Rōmānam.*

paulātim = gradually
alius, -a, -ud (irregular) = other
Aegyptus, -ī, f. = Egypt
restō, -āre, restitī = I am left
cūnctī, -ae, -a (plural) = all
prīnceps, prīncipis, m. = first, foremost man
quī = who
parcō, -ere, pepercī, parsum (+ dat.) (here) = I pardon
callidus, -a, -um = clever
urbānus, -a, -um (here) = tactful
nōn iam = no longer
annus, -ī, m. = year
pāx, pācis, f. = peace

Notes:
(i)   Note that *Aegyptus*, in common with the names of most islands, countries and cities, is feminine.
(ii) The Antony and Cleopatra mentioned here (line 3) are the famous stars of Shakespeare's play.
(iii) Augustus (line 9) is famous for having brought peace to the Roman world after years of civil war.

1.   Answer the following questions:

(a) In lines 1-2, say how Octavian got the better of other leaders.
(b) In line 3, who was Cleopatra?
(c) In line 4, who was Agrippa?
(d) In line 5, what kind of battle was the battle of Actium?
(e) *cūnctīs... parcit* (lines 6-7): what would you call Octavian for doing this?
(f) In lines 7-8, why do you think most people accepted Augustus as their leader?
(g) In line 9, to what was the name Octavianus changed?
(h) In lines 10-11, why do you think most men thought that Augustus was a 'good thing'?

2.   Translate the passage peacefully.

3. Answer the following questions:

    (a) *superat* (line 1): put this verb into the imperfect.
    (b) In line 2, if you had not just learnt *occīdit,* is there any other word you could have chosen to give this sense?
    (c) *sōlī* (line 2): give the genitive singular of this word.
    (d) In lines 4-5, how do the words *oppidum Graecum*, relate to the word *Actium*?
    (e) In line 5, give the principal parts (including the meaning) of the verb from which *vincit* comes.
    (f) In line 7, how does the form *callidissimus* relate to the adjective *callidus*?
    (g) *pulcherrimum* (line 10): put this into the comparative.
    (h) In lines 10-11, we are told that peace was given to men. If we wanted to say 'to a man', to what should we change *hominibus*?

Vocabulary 6

Vocabulary 6

antequam (+ verb) = before	*-que* = and
postquam (+ verb) = after	*occupō, -āre, -āvī, -ātum* = I seize (a place)
colligō, -ere, collēgī, collēctum = I collect	*flūmen, flūminis,* n. = river
dēfendō, -ere, dēfendī, dēfēnsum = I defend	*nōmen, nōminis,* n. = name
is, ea, id = that; he, she, it	*mōns, montis,* m. = mountain
quam = than	*pars, partis,* f. = part
urbs, urbis, f. = city	

We've made a big dent in our second half now; but let's sail on gallantly. (Forgive my mixed metaphors). For we are now about to learn why a bus is called a bus.

Chapter 7

3rd declension adjectives: trīstis

We start off straight away in this chapter with something you never even thought existed. Remember those adjectives ending in '-us' and '-er' which we learnt so many ages ago? They are called 2nd declension adjectives because their masculines – and neuters, for that matter – go like 2nd declension nouns. Well, these new adjectives are 3rd declension adjectives, going (pretty much) like 3rd declension nouns, and a large number of them end in '-is', like *trīstis*.

trīstis, trīste = 'sad', 'gloomy'			
Singular	**Masculine**	**Feminine**	**Neuter**
Nominative	*trīstis*	*trīstis*	*trīste*
Vocative	*trīstis*	*trīstis*	*trīste*
Accusative	*trīstem*	*trīstem*	*trīste*
Genitive	*trīstis*	*trīstis*	*trīstis*
Dative	*trīstī*	*trīstī*	*trīstī*
Ablative	*trīstī*	*trīstī*	*trīstī*
Plural			
Nominative	*trīstēs*	*trīstēs*	*trīstia*
Vocative	*trīstēs*	*trīstēs*	*trīstia*
Accusative	*trīstēs*	*trīstēs*	*trīstia*
Genitive	*trīstium*	*trīstium*	*trīstium*
Dative	*trīstibus*	*trīstibus*	*trīstibus*
Ablative	*trīstibus*	*trīstibus*	*trīstibus*

(i)   The masculine and feminine are identical throughout. The neuter makes a bid for independence in the first three cases, but toes the line in the last three.

(ii)   Beware of the ablative singular which, unlike that of the regular 3rd declension nouns, always ends in '-ī', thus being indistinguishable from the dative.

(iii)   These adjectives are regularly presented thus: *trīstis, trīste* = sad, gloomy. This gives the masculine (and feminine) form (*trīstis*), and the neuter (*trīste*). We often abbreviate the neuter form to '-e'. The stem of such adjectives is revealed straight away in the nominative singular by chopping off the *-is*, e.g. *trīst-*.

Like *trīstis* go:

crūdēlis, -e = cruel   *fortis, -e* = brave
difficilis, -e = difficult   *nōbilis, -e* = noble (of noble birth)
facilis, -e = easy   *omnis, -e* = all, every, whole (of)

Note how *facilis, -e* (from *faciō*) becomes *difficilis, -e* in the compound form. See our note on p. 56 on compound verbs. *omnis* is the commonest word for 'all'. In the singular it also means 'every' and 'the whole of'. For example Caesar's 'Gallic War' starts with the statement once known to every schoolboy throughout this country and many others, that the whole of Gaul was divided into three parts (*Gallia est omnis dīvīsa in partēs trēs*). From *omnis* comes our word *omnibus* (lit. 'for all', the dative plural), now shortened to 'bus'!

Exercise 7.1

Write out in full, as is shown above with *trīstis,* the declension of:

1. *difficilis, -e*
2. *facilis, -e*
3. *fortis, -e*
4. *omnis, -e*

Exercise 7.2

Translate into English:

1. *rēx fortibus mīlitibus dōna dabit.*
2. *dux crūdēlis multōs incolās vulnerāvit.*
3. *bene cantāre difficile est.*
4. *templum omne sacrum est.*
5. *paucī cīvēs nōbilēs erant.*
6. *hae mulierēs pulchrae erant.*
7. *itinera facilia semper fēcerat.*
8. *vīdēruntne crūdēlium hostium scūta?*
9. *hī senēs semper trīstēs sunt.*
10. *bene scrībere semper difficile est.*

Exercise 7.3

Translate into Latin:

1. It is difficult to conquer brave enemies.
2. All the leaders were of noble birth.
3. The happy boys were making an easy journey.
4. The whole* city is very beautiful. (*Use *omnis*.)
5. These are the soldiers of the cruel leaders.
6. They did not give gifts to the gloomy girl.
7. All farmers love good fields.
8. Men of noble birth are not always brave.
9. It is not easy to sing these words.
10. All men and all women wish to have brave leaders.

More on subordinate clauses

You will remember that it is nice to tuck subordinate clauses inside the sentence that they are in. If, for some reason, this won't work, then at least make sure that they do not come at the end, after the main verb. As we learnt in Book 1, the function of the main verb is to bind the whole sentence together; it doesn't always have to be the very last word in the sentence, but there should generally be no clause after it, i.e. no verb.

Consider the following sentence:
> 'Because the teacher was angry, the boys were afraid.'

This can be translated:
> *puerī, quod magister īrātus erat, timēbant.*

Or (less neatly):
> *quod magister īrātus erat, puerī timēbant.*

But it would not generally be good to write:

> *puerī timēbant quod magister īrātus erat.*

A subordinate clause trying to come after the main verb.

Note how we have coloured the subordinate clause in red so that you can easily see where it is in the sentence.

Exercise 7.4

Translate into Latin:

1. When the enemy seized the town, the citizens were afraid.
2. Although the youths were tired, they fought bravely.
3. I gave the slave nothing because he did not work.
4. We praise the boys and girls when they sing well.
5. The generals were angry because the soldiers were fleeing.
6. We gave gifts to the farmers because they built strong walls.
7. The maid-servants came quickly when the queen called them.
8. He hurried out of the city although he had eaten nothing.
9. Aulus remained with his companions because he loved them.
10. Everyone stood when the old men entered the temple.

Exercise 7.5

Translate into English:

1. *nostrōs gladiōs crūdēlēs mīlitēs capiunt.*
2. *fortēs puerī prō parvīs puellīs stābant.*
3. *virī nōbilēs ex urbe sine mulieribus nōn discessērunt.*
4. *sagittās in hoc oppidum iaciunt.*
5. *nōnne aurum omnēs cupiunt?*
6. *omnēs hostēs superāre difficile est.*
7. *agricolae in agrīs sub caelō labōrant.*
8. *difficile iter sine comitibus nōn faciam.*
9. *fortis dux prō cīvibus cum malīs hominibus pugnāvit.*
10. *bellum gerere numquam facile est.*

Vocabulary
prō + abl. = on behalf of, in front of, instead of
sine + abl. = without
sub + abl. = under

Exercise 7.6

Translate into Latin:

1. No one will depart from the mountain.
2. All the men were walking from the city to the temple.[1]
3. This brave old man is fighting on behalf of his country.
4. The whole city is safe because the enemy have departed.
5. The wicked boys are throwing books into the road.
6. The boys and girls are reading the books without their master.
7. All the citizens are fleeing from the city.[1]
8. Did a few soldiers really conquer these noble men?
9. Even[2] he, a king, is remaining under the wall.
10. Are not the enemy standing in front of the temple?

[1] *ex* is often right for 'from' when the meaning is obviously 'out of' just as *in* + acc. is right for 'to', when the meaning is obviously 'into'.

[2] Remember *etiam?*

Here's another nice (?) little thing. Don't mix up *forte* (= 'by chance') with *forte* (the neuter of *fortis*). In this case, quantities won't help. The words are identical, and we have to fall back on our old friend, the context; in other words, as I'm sure you remember, on common sense!

Exercise 7.7

Read the following passage carefully, and answer the questions on it.

The Roman Empire: from good to bad to worst

1　*post Augustum fuit Tiberius, quī paucissimōs amāvit; et*
　eum amāvērunt paucissimī; itaque multōs per annōs
　īnsulam Capreās habitābat, nec Rōmam veniēbat. post
　eum fuit C. Caesar (omnēs prīncipēs nōmen Caesaris*
5　*habuērunt); is, ubi parvus puer erat, parvās caligās*
　gerēbat; eum igitur omnēs Caligulam vocābant. Caligula,
　ubi prīnceps esse incēpit, bonus erat, sed mox, post
　morbum, erat saevus et crūdēlis. ōlim, ubi apud eum
　senātōrēs cēnābant, rīdēre incēpit nec cessāre potuit;
10　*et, ubi rogāvērunt Caligulam eī quī prope eum sedēbant,*
　'cūr rīdēs?' respondit eīs 'quod, sī cupiō, servōs meōs
　iubēre possum vōs statim occīdere.' illī quoque, quod
　eum magnopere timēbant, rīsērunt – sed simulātē.

qui = who
annus, -ī, m. = year
Capreae, -ārum, f. pl. = Capri
nec = and not, nor
C. = Gaius
prīnceps, prīncipis, m. = first, foremost man (see below)
caliga, -ae, f. = soldier's boot
gerō, -ere, gessī, gestum (here) = I wear
incipiō, incipere, incēpī, inceptum = I begin
morbus, -ī, m. = disease
apud + acc. = in the home of…
senātor, senātōris, m. = senator
cēnō, -āre, -āvī, -ātum = I dine
cessō, -āre, -āvī, -ātum = I stop (intr.)
sedeō, -ēre, sēdī, sessum = I sit
sī = if
simulātē = pretendedly, hollowly

* *Caesar* thus became a sort of title and gave birth to the German *Kaiser* and the Russian *Czar*.

Notes:

(i) *Caligula* (line 6) is a diminutive form of *caliga*, meaning 'little boot'. We might translate it as 'bootie'.

(ii) *prīnceps* (line 7) is the commonest word used to describe the 'top' man. It is often loosely translated as Emperor.

(iii) *incipiō* (line 7) is a compound of *capiō*. See note on p. 56.

(iv) *senātōrēs* (line 9): the senators were the highest ranking Roman officials.

1. Answer the following questions:

    (a) In lines 1-2, how would you describe Tiberius?
    (b) In lines 5-6, explain why Caligula was given his name?
    (c) In lines 6-8, was Caligula a good *prīnceps* for a long time?
    (d) Which word helped you to answer the above question? Translate this word.
    (e) In lines 12-13, why did Caligula's guests join in the laughter?
    (f) How would you have felt if you had been invited to dinner by Caligula?
    (g) What do you think of Caligula's sense of humour?

2. Translate the passage gingerly.

3. Answer the following questions:

    (a) *paucissimōs* (line 1): how does this relate to *paucōs*?
    (b) *Capreās* (line 3): how does this word relate to *īnsulam*?
    (c) In line 3, why is there no preposition before *Rōmam*?
    (d) *omnēs* (line 4): put this into the genitive plural.
    (e) Mention and translate all the infinitives in this passage.
    (f) *respondit* (line 11): if, instead of 'he replied', we had wanted to write 'they replied', what would we have written?
    (g) *eum* (line 13): put this word into the dative singular.

praenōmina

This may be a good place to say a few words about the Roman *praenōmen*. All Roman men had a *praenomen* (first name) ending in '*-us*'. The most common *praenōmina*, with their regular abbreviations, were as follows:

A.	= Aulus	M.	= Mārcus	Ser.	= Servius
C.	= Gāius	M'	= Mānius	Sp.	= Spurius
Cn.	= Gnaeus	P.	= Pūblius	T.	= Titus
D.	= Decimus	Q.	= Quīntus	Ti. (Tib.)	= Tiberius
L.	= Lūcius	S. (Sex.)	= Sextus		

Always translate these abbreviations (when you meet them) into the full names.

The rule given on page 22 about the pronunciation of words such as *huius* and *Troia* does not apply to the name *Gāius*. The '*a*' is long by nature and the '*i*' is a vowel. The name should thus be pronounced with three distinct syllables: *Gā-i-us*.

Exercise 7.8

*Let us now pay a visit, though uninvited, to the Pomponia family – *gēns Pompōnia* – and the Rabiria family – *gēns Rabīria* – and see how they get on with each other. Translate into English, giving abbreviated *praenomina* in full:

1. *P. Pompōnius M. Rabīriī amīcus est.*
2. *C. Rabīrius Cn. Pompōniō dōnum dedit.*
3. *D. Pompōnius cum P. Pompōniō in templum ambulat.*
4. *hic liber Cn. Pompōniī est.*
5. *ubi habitat M' Rabīrius?*
6. *T. Rabīrius propter verba L. Pompōniī laetus est.*
7. *vīditne herī Q. Pompōnius S. Rabīrium?*
8. *ō M. Rabīrī,* ubi est gladius Tib. Pompōniī?*
9. *ō P. Pompōnī,* cūr Ser. Rabīrium nōn laudās?*
10. *A. Rabīrius Sp. Pompōniō agrōs suōs ostendet.*

* Remember that the vocatives of names in *-ius* go like the vocative of *fīlius* (i.e. *fīlī*).

Exercise 7.9

Translate into Latin, giving the correct abbreviations for the *praenōmina*:

1. Aulus Pomponius did not fight with Titus Pomponius.
2. Gaius Rabirius always praises Tiberius Pomponius.
3. Is this really Quintus Pomponius' sword?
4. Where is Sextus Rabirius?
5. Both Marcus Pomponius and Gnaeus Rabirius have written books.
6. Oh! Decimus Rabirius, have you seen Manius Rabirius?
7. Oh! Servius Pomponius, are these the spears of Spurius Rabirius?
8. Lucius Rabirius and Aulus Pomponius are building a wall.
9. Gaius Pomponius is standing in front of Quintus Rabirius.
10. Marcus Rabirius is walking through the fields of Publius Pomponius.

ingēns

We haven't quite finished yet with 3rd declension adjectives. Some of these do not end in '*-is*' but in a consonant + '*s*' without any '*i*' in between, for example *ingēns.*

ingēns, ingentis = 'huge'

Singular

	Masculine	**Feminine**	**Neuter**
Nominative	*ingēns*	*ingēns*	*ingēns*
Vocative	*ingēns*	*ingēns*	*ingēns*
Accusative	*ingentem*	*ingentem*	*ingēns*
Genitive	*ingentis*	*ingentis*	*ingentis*
Dative	*ingentī*	*ingentī*	*ingentī*
Ablative	*ingentī*	*ingentī*	*ingentī*

Plural

	Masculine	Feminine	Neuter
Nominative	*ingentēs*	*ingentēs*	*ingentia*
Vocative	*ingentēs*	*ingentēs*	*ingentia*
Accusative	*ingentēs*	*ingentēs*	*ingentia*
Genitive	*ingentium*	*ingentium*	*ingentium*
Dative	*ingentibus*	*ingentibus*	*ingentibus*
Ablative	*ingentibus*	*ingentibus*	*ingentibus*

These third declension adjectives are also very tame. Their only eccentricity, if we can call it that, is that their neuter singular does not end in an '*e*'; in their accusative singular the rule that neuters are the same in nominative and accusative prevails. For the rest, note that, although these adjectives increase in the oblique cases, i.e. those other than the nominative and vocative, they form their genitive plurals in '*-ium*', like *trīstis*. The ablative singular ends in a long '*ī*', as does that of *trīstis*.

A number of these adjectives end in '*-x*'. Out of *fēlīx* and *audāx* we dig *fēlīc-* and *audāc-* as the stems on to which we add the endings.

These adjectives should be presented thus: *ingēns, ingentis* – huge

Like *ingēns* go:

audāx, audācis = bold
fēlīx, fēlīcis = lucky, happy, fortunate
sapiēns, sapientis = wise

Exercise 7.10

Write out in full:

1. *ingēns, ingentis* = huge
2. *audāx, audācis* = bold
3. *fēlīx, fēlīcis* = lucky
4. *sapiēns, sapientis* = wise

Comparison of 3rd declension adjectives

Here again is good news about something that is surprisingly straightforward.

Third declension adjectives form their comparatives and superlatives in exactly the same way as second declension adjectives do. For example, the comparative of *trīstis* is *trīstior* and the superlative is *trīstissimus*. Similarly, '*-ior*' and '*-issimus*' are added to '*ingent-*', '*audāc-*', '*fēlīc-*' and '*sapient-*'. And these forms decline in exactly the same way as *laetior* and *laetissimus* do from *laetus*.

Well, it isn't quite as easy as all that. You could hardly expect it to be, could you? One might almost begin to get suspicious, if there wasn't a little hiccough somewhere! The superlative of *facilis* is *facillimus* and the superlative of *difficilis* is *difficillimus*. And these two words are immensely common.

Exercise 7.11

Translate into English:

1. *hoc iter facilius erit illō.*
2. *facillimum iter laudāmus.*
3. *in templum ingēns intrāverant.*
4. *audācēs virōs numquam amābō.*
5. *iuvenis ille audācissimus mīlitem gladiō vulnerāvit.*
6. *dī fēlīcī puerō bona dōna dedērunt.*
7. *hic mōns illīs montibus ingentior est.*
8. *paucī sapientiōrēs fuērunt Solōne.*
9. *hanc urbem, quamquam eam fortissimī mīlitēs oppugnābant, mūrus servāvit.*
10. *dux fortis ducem crūdēlem superāvit.*

Exercise 7.12

Translate into Latin:

1. The brave citizens were defending the city wall.
2. A huge wind destroyed the whole temple.
3. These old men are very brave because they are fighting with the bold soldiers.
4. These youths are wiser than those because they stayed in the city.
5. The lucky girl is preparing the food.
6. Who is the wisest of men?
7. One bold leader saved all the inhabitants.
8. Our parents used to warn us about all the dangers.
9. Didn't the cruel masters punish you, Aemilia?
10. Did the war really destroy all this land?

It's time for another story. I thought we'd leave Caligula for the moment but return soon to him and his strange successor, Claudius. For the time being, though, let's go back many a century to the siege of Troy – we can say around 1250 B.C. for the sake of argument – and see the Greeks through their various ordeals.

Exercise 7.13

Read the following passage carefully and answer the questions on it.

The Trojan War: the Greeks are detained in Aulis

1　poētae Graecī et Rōmānī haec dē bellō Troiānō
　　scrīpsērunt: Menelāus rēx fuit Spartae; eum vīsit Paris,
　　fīlius Priamī, quī Troiam regēbat. Paris Helenam Menelāī
　　uxōrem, quae pulcherrima erat, cēpit et cum eā Troiam
5　discessit. Menelāus, quī eam recipere cupīvit, ad frātrem
　　suum vēnit, Agamemnonem, et eum auxilium rogāvit.
　　Agamemnōn rēx fuit omnium Graecōrum, et ducēs
　　omnēs ad bellum vocāvit; hī cum mīlitibus suīs prope
　　locum nōmine Aulidem convēnērunt; inde Troiam
10　nāvigāre cōnstituerant, sed Agamemnōn deam Diānam
　　offenderat; et dea Graecōs omnēs sīc pūnīvit: ventum
　　secundum eīs nōn dabat, et diūtissimē Graecī, quod
　　nāvigāre nōn poterant, in ūnō locō manēbant īrātissimī.

vīsō, -ere, vīsī, vīsum = I visit
quī (m.), quae (f.) = who
recipiō, -ere, recēpī, receptum
　= I take back
Aulis, -idis, f. = Aulis
conveniō, -īre, convēnī,
　conventum = I meet, come
　together
inde = thence, from there
offendō, -ere, offendī,
　offēnsum (here) = I offend
secundus, -a, -um (here) =
　favourable
diūtissimē = for a very long time

Notes:

(i)　Priamī (line 3): we generally refer to Priamus by the English form Priam.

(ii)　recipiō (line 5) is a compound verb (see p. 56). conveniō (line 9) is a compound of cum + veniō. Note how cum generally becomes con in compounds.

1.　Answer the following questions:

　(a) In lines 1-2, how do we know about the Trojan War?
　(b) Menelāus… cēpit (lines 2-4): mention everything we learn about Menelaus.
　(c) In lines 5-6, what made Menelaus visit his brother?
　(d) In line 7, why was Agamemnon so important?
　(e) In lines 8-9, what did the Greek leaders do near Aulis?
　(f) In lines 10-11, why did Diana punish the Greeks?
　(g) In lines 11-12, how did Diana punish the Greeks?
　(h) In line 13, which word tells us what the Greeks felt about all this?

2.　Translate the passage frustratedly.

3.   Answer the following questions:

(a) *eum* (line 2): what is the dative singular of this word?
(b) In line 4, why is there no preposition in front of *Troiam*?
(c) *discessit* (line 5): put this verb into the pluperfect.
(d) *cupīvit* (line 5): give the principal parts, including the meaning of this word.
(e) In line 6, if, instead of *vēnit* we read *venit,* what would this mean?
(f) In line 8, if, instead of 'with their own soldiers' we wished to say 'without their own soldiers', how would we have to change the words *cum mīlitibus suīs*?
(g) In line 8, if, instead of 'their own' soldiers, we wanted to say 'their (other men's)' soldiers, what would we write instead of *suīs*?
(h) *quod... poterant* (line 12-13): what sort of clause is this? Explain its position in the sentence.

Notes:

(i)   *Troiānus* (line 1) (= 'Trojan') and *Troia* (line 3) (= 'Troy') were originally spelt *Troiiānus* and *Troiia*, the two 'i's being consonantal like two English 'y's as in 'y-yes'! Although one of the 'i's was dropped in the spelling, thc first syllable of each word remained as a long syllable and should accordingly be lingered on: but the '*o*' is not long by nature and should not be pronounced as such. See p. 22 on *huius.*

(ii)   Sparta (line 2) was an important Greek city in the Peloponnese (the southern part of Greece).

(iii) *Helena* (line 3), Menelaus' wife, is of course the famous Helen of Troy who 'launched a thousand ships'.

(iv)   *Aulis* (line 9) was a sea-port in *Boeōtia*, a district north of Athens.

(v)   A number of different reasons have been given for Diana's anger with the Greeks (lines 10-11). I have therefore chosen to be rather vague on the subject.

Exercise 7.14

Match up the Latin words 1-5 with the English ones a-e. Explain the connexion between the Latin and the English ones.

1.	*crūdēlis*	(a)	fortitude
2.	*difficilis*	(b)	nobility
3.	*nōbilis*	(c)	difficult
4.	*omnis*	(d)	cruel
5.	*fortis*	(e)	omnipotent

And here are some easy sentences together with some others:

Exercise 7.15

Translate into Latin:

1.   The good queen was warning the wicked inhabitants.
2.   The happy boys are singing new words.
3.   The savage sailors were frightening the beautiful girl.
4.   The strong farmer is setting free a few horses.
5.   The Greek teacher was praising the rest of the boys.

6. This huge place is gloomier than that one.
7. This bold boy is very lucky.
8. Weren't the wretched old men warning the little girls?
9. Did the very brave soldiers really overcome the most cruel general?
10. Were all the citizens really praising those leaders?

Vocabulary 7

Vocabulary 7

crūdēlis, -e = cruel	*audāx, -ācis* = bold
difficilis, -e = difficult	*fēlīx, -īcis* = lucky
facilis, -e = easy	*ingēns, -entis* = huge
fortis, -e = brave	*sapiēns, -entis* = wise
nōbilis, -e = noble	*forte* = by chance
trīstis, -e = sad, gloomy	*quamquam* = though, although
omnis, -e = all, every	

Oh dear! Once again we're getting dangerously near the end.

Chapter 8

More irregular comparisons

Let's start this chapter with some more irregular comparatives and superlatives:

Positive	Comparative	Superlative
magnus	*maior*	*maximus*
parvus	*minor*	*minimus*

The comparatives decline like *peior* (see page 63), and the superlatives decline like *bonus*, so we have no problems there. For the pronunciation of *maior* see note on *huius* on page 22.

In many schools, particularly prep and public schools, when two brothers are at the school at the same time, the boys are called by their surname with the addition of (ma) or (mi) – short for *maior* or *minor*.

e.g.   Oulton (ma) is older than Oulton (mi).

If a third Oulton brother were to arrive, he would be called Oulton (min) – short for *minimus*. Finally, if a fourth Oulton brother were to arrive (bankrupting his poor family in the process), everyone would move up a place, giving the following hierarchy of Oultons:

Oulton (max) – short for *maximus*
Oulton (ma)
Oulton (mi)
Oulton (min)

You will notice that I talk here of brothers rather than sisters. This is because, in the days when such customs were developed in schools, brothers and sisters would almost certainly not have been at the same school; and in any case girls have tended to be treated more respectfully than boys, with the use of their first names rather than all these 'ma's, 'mi's, and 'min's.

A very common use of *maior* crops up in the plural *maiōrēs* which was used to mean 'ancestors'. We hear a lot about *maiōrēs nostrī*; also about something (e.g. a punishment, often a particularly nasty one) being carried out *mōre maiōrum*. *mōre* is the ablative of *mōs, mōris*, m. = 'custom, way'; and the expression means 'in the way of our ancestors'.

So, having sorted out the Oulton family, and the gruesome ways of the Romans' ancestors, we shall begin with some exercises on *maior*.

maximus　　*maior*　　*minor*　　*minimus*

Exercise 8.1

Translate into English:

1. *estne hic maiōris hominis gladius?*
2. *quis maior est quam Augustus?*
3. *estne hic puer hāc puellā maior?*
4. *ille magnum oppidum habitat, sed ego maius habitō.*
5. *nōnne mare quam flūmina maius est?*
6. *eius dōna maiōra sunt quam mea.*
7. *crās cum maiōribus iuvenibus ad montem festīnābō.*
8. *hae hastae maiōrum hominum sunt.*
9. *Aulus gladium maiōrem habet quam ego.*
10. *Laelia trēs sorōrēs maiōrēs nōn amat.*

Exercise 8.2

Translate into Latin:

1. Aulus is bigger than his (own) brother.
2. Who is greater than Alexander?[1]
3. You have a big horse, but I have a bigger one.
4. I hurried to the town with the bigger boys.
5. Isn't our city bigger than yours, farmers?
6. Soldier, give this big sword to that bigger youth.
7. Those old men are bigger than these women.
8. Is there really a greater poet than Homer?[2]
9. Those soldiers have bigger spears than our leader.
10. All the citizens were standing in the bigger town; they were laughing.

[1] *Alexander, Alexandrī*, m. – King of Macedon, known as 'The Great'. He lived from 356-323 B.C. and conquered most of the known world, dying at the age of 33 from fever.

[2] *Homērus, -ī*, m. – regarded as the author of the *Iliad* and *Odyssey*, the two great epics of Ancient Greece. His exact identity remains obscure; he may have been blind, and he may have lived in the 8th century B.C.

And now for some practice at *maximus*.

Exercise 8.3

Translate into English:

1. *hōs virōs, maximōs cīvium, vidē!*
2. *quis omnium poētārum maximus est?*
3. *in hāc īnsulā, ille ager maximus est.*
4. *maxima templa in maximīs urbibus sunt.*
5. *in hāc terrā ducēs maximī habitant.*
6. *quis hunc maximum omnium librōrum legere cupit?*
7. *hostēs in oppidum nostrum sagittās maximās iēcērunt.*
8. *portatne maximus ille mīles maximās hastās?*
9. *nōnne hic dux mīles maximus est?*
10. *num hic mīles dux maximus est?*

Exercise 8.4

Translate into Latin:

1. Julius Caesar was the greatest of the Roman leaders.
2. Aulus, are there very wise and very great old men in your city?
3. In my fatherland, this temple is the biggest.
4. Very big sailors were fighting with very big farmers on the very big island.
5. I shall give the biggest book to the biggest boy.
6. These are the swords of the biggest soldiers.
7. The old men will give big gifts to the biggest youths.
8. This is the name of the very great woman.
9. We all praised the very great poet.
10. No one loved the very great leader because he was cruel.

And now for some work on *minor*. Note that in English a minor is someone less or younger than a certain age (not to be confused with a miner, who digs under ground), and a minor poet is a lesser poet.

Exercise 8.5

Translate into English:

You must be the minor min...

1. *nōnne hic magnus puer equō minor est?*
2. *hoc oppidum minus est quam illa urbs.*
3. *in parvā īnsulā templa minōra sunt.*
4. *eius fīlia fīliō minor est.*
5. *huic mīlitī minōrem gladium dā!*
6. *num hī iuvenēs quam illī senēs minōrēs sunt?*
7. *illīus frāter minor est quam soror.*
8. *hic homō fīliā suā minor est.*
9. *Aulus et Mārcus minōrēs sunt parentibus.*
10. *haec flūmina minōra illīs sunt.*

Exercise 8.6

Translate into Latin:

1. This queen is smaller than all her maid-servants.
2. Give this little book to a smaller girl, Marcus!
3. There were two brothers: the greater and the lesser.
4. That island is smaller than this city.
5. Which of these poets is the lesser?
6. Is this field really the smaller farmer's?
7. Aren't these ships smaller than those?
8. His mother is smaller than his daughter.
9. His friends always give him the smaller spear.
10. Those mountains are smaller than these, aren't they?

And now, finally, to a section on *minimus*.

Exercise 8.7

Translate into English:

1. *meōrum fīliōrum hic minimus est.*
2. *in hāc urbe minima puella pulcherrima est.*
3. *num minimī mīlitēs bene pugnant?*
4. *hoc omnium nostrōrum templōrum minimum est.*
5. *nōnne minimī puerī fortissimē prō patriā pugnant?*
6. *hic magister semper magnopere minimās puellās laudat.*
7. *in hōc oppidō minimī iuvenēs maximīs senibus maiōrēs sunt.*
8. *hic liber minimī puerī est.*
9. *dux ad īnsulam in nāve minimā nāvigāvit.*
10. *hic est frāter meus: minimus est.*

By the way, the adverb *minimē* is very commonly used to mean 'no'.

e.g. *'amāsne hunc puerum, Laelia?'*
  'minimē!'
The Latin for 'yes' is *ita* (= 'thus'), or *ita vērō* (= 'thus truly').

Exercise 8.8

Translate into Latin:

num illum amās?

minimē!

1. Who is the smallest boy here?
2. The queen gave gifts to the least of her maid-servants.
3. This boy and his brother are very small, aren't they?
4. Do these swords really belong to* the smallest youths?
5. 'Oh! slave, do you really love your cruel master?' 'No!'
6. Even the least of poets can write well.
7. 'Didn't the smallest citizens run quickly?' 'No!'
8. The teacher gave the girls very small presents.

*Think carefully about how to cope with this one. To give you a clue, you will need a genitive.

We have one more particularly vicious comparative up our sleeve, but we shall save it for a while, so that you can look forward to it. But now the time has come to continue our story about the Greeks being detained in Aulis on their way to Troy. Poor old Agamemnon; it isn't always fun being at the head of everything and therefore being responsible for everything. In this particular story you will see how terribly true this is.

Exercise 8.9

The Trojan War: Agamemnon hears Calchas' prophecy

1   *tandem Agamemnōn <u>vātem</u> vocāvit nōmine <u>Calchantem</u>*
   et rogāvit eum 'quis nōs sīc pūnit?' respondit ille 'dea
   Diāna, quod tū eam <u>offendistī</u>, vōs pūnit.' rogāvit iterum
   Agamemnōn, 'quid igitur nunc facere <u>dēbeō</u>?' respondit
5   *<u>vātēs</u>, 'tū filiam tuam deae <u>sacrificāre</u> <u>dēbēs</u> Īphigenīam.'*
   Agamemnōn miserrimus fuit et tandem nūntium mīsit
   <u>Mycēnās</u>; ibi habitābat uxor eius Clytaemnēstra; is, ubi
   <u>advēnit</u>, 'rēx,' dīxit, 'Agamemnōn tē iubet, ō rēgīna,
   <u>Aulidem</u> cum filiā tuā venīre Īphigenīa; nam illa <u>nūbere</u>
10   *<u>dēbet</u> <u>Achillī</u>.' Clytaemnēstra igitur laetissima fuit; nam*
   Achillēs ille et fortissimus erat ducum Graecōrum et
   nōbilissimus. <u>Aulidem</u> rēgīna statim cum filiā festīnāvit.

vātēs, vātis, c. (here) = prophet
Calchās, Calchantis, m. =
   Calchas (a prophet)
offendō, -ere, offendī,
   offēnsum = I offend
dēbeō, -ēre, -uī, -itum (+ infin.)
   = I must, ought
sacrificō, -āre, -āvī, -ātum =
   I sacrifice
Mycēnae, -ārum, f. pl. =
   Mycenae (a town in
   Greece)
adveniō, -īre, advēnī, adventum
   = I arrive
Aulis, Aulidis, f. = Aulis
nūbō, -ere, nūpsī, nūptum
   (+ dat.) = I marry
Achillēs, -is, m. = Achilles

Note:
The verb *nūbō* (line 9) is used to describe a woman marrying a man, not a man marrying a woman.

1.   Answer the following questions:

    (a) In line 1-2, what did Agamemnon ask Calchas?
    (b) In lines 3-5, why did Agamemnon become so wretched?
    (c) In lines 6-7, why did he send a messenger to Mycenae?
    (d) In lines 8-10, was the message sent to Clytemnestra true or false? Answer in full.
    (e) Why did Agamemnon send this message?
    (f) In lines 10-12, why was Clytemnestra so pleased with the message?
    (g) Comment on Agamemnon's behaviour in this story down to *Īphigenīam* in line 5.
    (h) Comment on Agamemnon's behaviour in this story from *Agamemnōn* in line 6 down to
       the end.

2.   Translate the passage prophetically.

3.   Answer the following questions:

    (a) *nōmine* (line 1): what case is this word? Translate it.
    (b) *dea... pūnit* (lines 2-3): comment on the order of words in Calchas' answer.
    (c) *respondit* (line 4): put this verb into the future tense.
    (d) *filiam* (line 5): what is the ablative plural of this word?
    (e) In line 7, why is there no word for 'to' before *Mycēnās*?
    (f) *uxor* (line 7): can you think of a synonym (in Latin) for this word?
    (g) *ducum* (line 11): is this genitive plural regular? Explain your answer.
    (h) If, in line 12, rather than 'she hurried', we wished to say 'she had hurried', what would
       festīnāvit become?

A couple of gems

This story will soon be continued. But first, here are a few nice little things:

(i)   *mī :* the vocative, masculine of *meus* (= 'my') is *mī:* hence 'Oh my son' is '*ō mī fīlī*' and 'Oh my friend' is '*ō mī amīce*'. Beware, however, that sometimes *mī* is a short form of *mihi*, the dative singular of *ego* = 'to (or for) me'.

(ii)   Questions introduced by *nōnne* or *num* can often be best translated by emphatic statements, with or without the addition of a little question such as 'is he?' or 'isn't he?'

e.g.   *nōnne fortissimus est hic mīles?* could be translated:
        'Surely this soldier is very brave (isn't he?)'

e.g.   *num parvus puer hunc mīlitem superāvit?* could be rendered:
        'Surely a little boy has not overcome this soldier (has he?)'

Exercise 8.10

Translate into English:

1.   *ō frāter mī, et magnus et validus es.*
2.   *nōnne scūta omnia ducī ostendērunt?*
3.   *nōnne puerī hōs librōs lēgērunt?*
4.   *num nautās omnēs saevae undae occīdērunt?*
5.   *ō mī domine, servōs tuōs dēfende.*
6.   *illud oppidum hostēs dēlēvērunt.*
7.   *ō mī fīlī, bene cantās.*
8.   *nūntium ad rēgem mīsērunt.*
9.   *nōnne nōs fortissimī ducēs dūcunt?*
10.   *ō mī pater, cūr miserrimus es?*

Exercise 8.11

Translate into Latin:

1.   Quintus, the poet, wrote these very beautiful words, didn't he?
2.   You are now very strong, my boy.
3.   A huge wind has destroyed that wall.
4.   Surely this mountain is higher than that (one), isn't it?
5.   After the girls had worked for a long time, they were tired.
6.   Surely the little boy didn't throw this arrow, did he?
7.   Oh! my son, you are not very wise.
8.   Marcus is Aulus' friend, and loves his (Aulus') sister.
9.   Sextus has often advised his (own) brother about the dangers.
10.   Oh! my friend, surely you will come soon to this town, won't you?

Let's have a little interlude now with adverbs, which have been left out in the cold for a long time.

The formation of adverbs

An adverb qualifies a verb in much the same way as an adjective describes a noun: it tells us 'how' or 'in what manner' the verb is done. To form an adverb from an adjective in English we regularly add 'ly' to the adjective: hence 'badly', 'accurately', 'boldly'. In Latin, it is similarly straight-forward: in the case of 1st/2nd declension adjectives, we just add *-ē* to the stem (found in the genitive singular by chopping off the *-ī* ending):

Adjective	Adverb	Meaning
clārus (stem *clār-*)	*clārē*	clearly
miser (stem *miser-*)	*miserē*	wretchedly
pulcher (stem *pulchr-*)	*pulchrē*	beautifully

The adverbs *fortiter* (= bravely) and *celeriter* (= quickly) are formed from 3rd declension adjectives. As for *bene* (= well), we have already learned this one without too much trouble. And when we think that the adverb from 'good' in English is 'well' (rather than 'goodly'!), we can't really complain about it. Good (!) old English!

The comparison of adverbs

Just as we have a comparative and a superlative of an adjective, so it is with adverbs. Thus from 'wretchedly' we get 'more wretchedly' and 'very wretchedly'. Armed with this knowledge, here is something pretty useful, followed by something very useful.

(i)   The adverb of the comparative is always regular; it is the same form as the neuter singular of the comparative adjective:

Adjective	Comparative adjective	Adverb	Comparative adverb
clārus, -a, -um	*clārior, clārius*	*clārē*	*clārius*
miser, -a, -um	*miserior, miserius*	*miserē*	*miserius*
pulcher, -chra, -chrum	*pulchrior, pulchrius*	*pulchrē*	*pulchrius*

(ii)   The adverb of the superlative is even more gloriously easy and regular; it is the superlative of the adjective with *-ē* instead of *-us*:

Adjective	Superlative adjective	Adverb	Superlative adverb
clārus, -a, -um	*clārissimus, -a, -um*	*clārē*	*clārissimē*
miser, -a, -um	*miserrimus, -a, -um*	*miserē*	*miserrimē*
pulcher, -chra, -chrum	*pulcherrimus, -a, -um*	*pulchrē*	*pulcherrimē*

While we are on the subject of superlative adverbs, we shall meet the superlative form from the adverb *celeriter* in this book, in a rather wonderful and useful phrase:

quam celerrimē = 'as quickly as possible.'

In fact, the Romans were far more expansive than we are and loved superlatives; so these forms can often solve our problems when we are putting English into Latin.

Exercise 8.12

Translate into English:

1. *iuvenēs in urbem celeriter cucurrērunt.*
2. *senēs cum hostibus fortiter pugnābant.*
3. *hunc mūrum agricolae celerrimē aedificāvērunt.*
4. *nostram urbem fortissimē dēfendēbāmus.*
5. *hī puerī quam celerrimē in urbem festīnāvērunt.*

Exercise 8.13

Translate into Latin:

1. These citizens are running as quickly as possible.
2. The girls sang these words well.
3. The youths defended the city bravely.
4. The winds quickly destroyed the ships.
5. The boys ate the food as quickly as possible.

Prohibitions

Back to verbs again. I warned you. After all, they are the most important parts of speech. The word 'verb' comes from *verbum* = 'a word'! They are so arrogant that they regard themselves as words *par excellence*. (Forgive me for showing off my French, which, to tell you the truth, isn't all that wonderful.) So then, here's a splendid, completely new construction – a prohibition – which is used when we wish to give a **negative command**, for example 'don't run!' or 'don't shout!' To do this, we use either *nōlī* (singular) or *nōlīte* (plural), followed by an infinitive. These forms come from a very irregular verb, which we shall learn in Book 3 (note how we are beginning to set our sights on the future); this verb is *nōlō,* and it means 'I do not wish'.

e.g. *nōlī hoc facere, puer!* = 'do not wish to do this, boy!' (i.e. 'do not do this, boy!')
nōlīte hoc facere, puerī! = 'do not wish to do this, boys!' (i.e. 'do not do this, boys!')

We shall see how the rest of the verb *nōlō* behaves in Book 3, but for now, make sure you recognise and know how to use *nōlī* and *nōlīte* and you will be fine.

Exercise 8.14

Translate into English:

1. *nōlī cantāre!*
2. *nōlīte clāmāre!*
3. *puerī, in templō lūdere nōlīte!*
4. *ō magister, nōlī malōs iuvenēs laudāre!*
5. *nōlī, saeve nauta, miserum equum vulnerāre!*
6. *ō cīvēs, nōlīte timēre hostēs!*
7. *ō rēgīna, ancillās terrēre nōlī!*
8. *ex īnsulā, incolae, fugere nōlīte!*
9. *ō mī fīlī, nōlī malōrum cīvium amīcus esse!*
10. *nōlīte, ō iuvenēs, mē sōlum relinquere!*

Exercise 8.15

Translate into Latin:

1. Do not run (singular)!
2. Do not walk (plural)!
3. Citizens, do not kill these horses!
4. Little boy, do not fight with the girls!
5. Farmers, do not flee from the fields!
6. Do not remain in the city, old men!
7. Do not run quickly, my son!
8. Do not depart from our town, bravest of leaders!
9. Oh my son, do not eat the food!
10. Oh wicked boys, do not frighten me!

It's time for us now to return to the sad story of Iphigenia, the daughter of Agamemnon and Clytemnestra.

Exercise 8.16

The Trojan War: the fate of Iphigenia

1　*advēnērunt <u>Aulidem</u> Clytaemnēstra et Īphigenīa. timēbat*
　Agamemnōn dīcere uxōrī <u>id quod</u> <u>vērum</u> erat; sed haec
　illud mox <u>cognōvit</u>. tum māter miserrima coniugī suō
　dīcēbat, 'nōlī fīliam nostram <u>sacrificāre</u>!' sed frāter
5　*Menelāus '<u>recipe</u> uxōrem meam!' dīcēbat; et ducēs*
　Graecī, 'dūc nōs,' clāmābant, 'dūc nōs sine morā Troiam!'
　tum dīxit Īphigenīa Agamemnonī 'ō pater, fac <u>id quod</u>
　facere <u>dēbēs</u>! mortem nōn timeō.' et occīdere eam
　cōnstituit pater miserrimus. et statim ventus <u>secundus</u>
10　*fuit. deinde Troiam nāvigāvērunt Graecī, sed <u>Mycēnās</u>*
　sōla <u>revēnit</u> Clytaemnēstra miserrima et īrātissima. et ubi,
　post decem <u>annōs</u>, Troiam cēpit Agamemnōn et laetus in
　patriam <u>revēnit</u>, statim eum uxor in <u>balneō</u> necāvit.

Aulis, Aulidis, f. = Aulis
id quod = that which
vērus, -a, -um = true
cognōscō, -ere, cognōvī,
　cognitum = I get to know
sacrificō, -āre, -āvī, -ātum =
　I sacrifice
recipiō, recipere, recēpī,
　receptum = I take back
dēbeō, -ēre, dēbuī, dēbitum
　(+ infin.) = I must, ought
secundus, -a, -um (here) =
　favourable
Mycēnae, -ārum, f. pl. =
　Mycenae
reveniō, -īre, revēnī, reventum =
　I come back
annus, -ī, m. = year
balneum, -ī, n. = bath

The Roman poet Lucretius (c. 94-55 B.C.) in his great poem 'Concerning the nature of things', describes in harrowing language the slaughter of Iphigenia; but the Greek tragedian Euripides (485-406? B.C.), in his wonderful play 'Iphigenia in Aulis', has her rescued by Artemis at the last moment. Different writers had different views about this whole story – as is so often the case.

1. Answer the following questions:

    (a) In line 2, how can we translate *id quod vērum erat* briefly and neatly?
    (b) In lines 3-6, how would you describe Agamemnon's plight?
    (c) In lines 7-8 what was Iphigenia's response to her father?
    (d) In lines 7-8, what do you think of this response?
    (e) In lines 8-9, what did Agamemnon decide to do?
    (f) In lines 10-11, which word makes you feel particularly sorry for Clytemnestra here?
    (g) In line 12, why was Agamemnon *laetus*?
    (h) In line 13, do you think Agamemnon got the treatment he deserved? Answer in full.

2. Translate the passage sadly.

3. Answer the following questions:

    (a) In line 1, why is *advēnērunt* plural?
    (b) In line 2, what is the case and gender of *haec*?
    (c) In line 3, what is the case and gender of *illud*?
    (d) In line 6, put *clāmābant* into the pluperfect.
    (e) In line 7 we are told that 'Iphigenia said…' If, instead of 'she said', we wanted to say 'she will say', to what should *dīxit* be changed?
    (f) In line 10, put *fuit* into the plural.
    (g) In line 10, why is there no preposition before *Troiam* or before *Mycēnās*?
    (h) *sōla* (line 11): what is the genitive singular of this word?

Here are some useful verbs:

accipiō, accipere, accēpi, acceptum	= I receive
adveniō, advenīre, advēnī, adventum	= I arrive, come to
effugiō, effugere, effūgī	= I escape
inveniō, invenīre, invēnī, inventum	= I find (lit. come upon)
redūcō, redūcere, redūxī, reductum	= I lead back

These are all compound verbs, i.e. a simple verb preceded by a preposition or by '*re-*'. We have had some of these already, but this may be a good moment to say a bit more about them. For example, *accipiō* is *ad* + *capiō* (for compounds of verbs with a short '*a*' in the stem, see p. 56). As for *ad* changing to '*ac*' we have something similar in *effugiō,* where the *ex* has changed to '*ef*': it simply makes the word easier to say. With *veniō, ad* and *in* behave respectably and in *redūcō,* the '*re*' has its usual meaning of 'back'.

Exercise 8.17

Translate into English:

1.   *ubi advēnī, nihil invēnī.*
2.   *cīvēs, ubi hostēs ad urbem advēnērunt, eōs effūgērunt.*
3.   *mulierēs nostrās malī nautae cēpērunt; et eās quam celerrimē redūcere cupimus.*
4.   *effugientne nautās puellae?*
5.   *pulcherrimum dōnum dux fortis accēpit.*
6.   *nōnne multam pecūniam in oppidō invēnistis?*
7.   *virīs mulierēs et cibum et vīnum dedērunt.*
8.   *puerōs ab hostibus tutōs quam celerrimē redūcēmus.*
9.   *cīvēs, postquam hostēs urbī appropinquāvērunt, eōs effugere cōnstituērunt.*
10. *num aurum in agrō invēnistī?*

Exercise 8.18

Translate into Latin:

1. Did you really escape from the enemy as quickly as possible, Titus?
2. Today I shall receive many gifts.
3. I found this little girl in the field yesterday.
4. Tomorrow we shall arrive at the town.
5. Who led the old men back from the island?
6. The slaves escaped the anger of their master.
7. My companions received much money yesterday.
8. He arrived at the town with me.
9. I shall lead the women back to Rome tomorrow.
10. We found the rest of the spears after the battle.

Exercise 8.19

Of what English words do the following Latin ones remind you? Explain the connexion between the words you have chosen and the Latin words.

1. *inveniō*
2. *accipiō*
3. *audāx*
4. *fēlīx*

Exercise 8.20

Translate into Latin:

1. The good masters were warning the slaves.
2. The angry teachers are not praising the bad boys.
3. The little girls have much gold.
4. The strong farmers were building a high wall.
5. The poet was looking at the beautiful temple.
6. The cruel enemy were attacking the city.
7. Savage winds destroyed the temples yesterday.
8. The terrified inhabitants escaped from the soldiers.
9. The masters punished their wicked slaves.
10. The very brave youths have saved the wretched old men.

Vocabulary 8

Vocabulary 8
accipiō, accipere, accēpī, acceptum = I receive
adveniō, -īre, advēnī, adventum = I arrive
effugiō, effugere, effūgī = I escape
inveniō, -īre, invēnī, inventum = I find
occīdō, -ere, occīdī, occīsum = I kill
redūcō, -ere, redūxī, reductum = I lead back
trādō, -ere, trādidī, trāditum = I hand over

celeriter = quickly
mors, mortis, f. = death
tum = then
*autem** = however, but, moreover
et...et = both...and
nōlī/nōlīte (+ infin.) = do not...!

* *autem* should not be first word in sentence.

And now for Chapter 9, which is a real stunner.

Chapter 9

eō = I go

You may have noticed that there's one very important verb which we haven't dealt with yet and for which we have constantly had to use various circumlocutions. Yes, there's only one possibility really – it's the verb 'to go'. As you had probably guessed, it's something of an outsider, or we'd have had it years ago. Funnily enough, the only verb we've had yet which can compare with it for weirdness is our dear old friend *sum.* But we learnt that long ago, when we didn't really know what 'irregular' meant. We do now, so be brave; once again, sit firm and behold!

eō, īre, iī or īvī, itum = 'I go'

Present tense

1st person singular	*eō*	I go, am going, do go
2nd person singular	*īs*	you (sing.) go, are going, do go
3rd person singular	*it*	he, she, it goes, is going, does go
1st person plural	*īmus*	we go, are going, do go
2nd person plural	*ītis*	you (plur.) go, are going, do go
3rd person plural	*eunt*	they go, are going, do go

Well, perhaps it's not quite as bad as all that! The inside parts are regular 4th conjugation, but the two outside parts in which they are wrapped are certainly strange. Note also that the supine *itum* has a short '*i*', unlike that of *audiō*. And now for the imperfect, which is surprisingly straightforward.

Imperfect tense

1st person singular	*ībam*	I was going, used to go
2nd person singular	*ībās*	you (sing.) were going, used to go
3rd person singular	*ībat*	he, she, it was going, used to go
1st person plural	*ībāmus*	we were going, used to go
2nd person plural	*ībātis*	you (plur.) were going, used to go
3rd person plural	*ībant*	they were going, used to go

Although this is not like *audiō,* which went *audiēbam* (remember?), it has a clear and honest logic of its own.

Exercise 9.1

Copy out in full the present and imperfect tenses of *eō,* as above, and say them either to yourself or aloud so many times that you know them irrevocably by heart. This means, as one of my old teachers used to tell us, that if you were woken up brutally at 3 a.m. and asked, while still half asleep, to go through these two tenses, you would do so correctly without a second's hesitation.

Compounds of eō

So now that we know these tenses, totally and utterly, before we advance to the others, let's look at some compounds of *eō*. In fact *eō* positively bristles with compounds; and here are a few of the commoner ones:

exeō = I go out
ineō = I go in or enter (transitive and intransitive)
pereō = (a bit unexpectedly) I perish
*redeō** = I return (intransitive), go back
trānseō = I cross (transitive and intransitive)

*N.B. The '*d*' here is brought in for the sake of euphony, which means 'pleasant sound' – i.e. *redeō* is more pleasant to say and hear than '*re-eō*' would be. Incidentally, don't mix up euphony with euphemism, which means the use of a mild expression in place of a stark or coarse one: e.g. 'to pass away' is a euphemism for 'to die'.

Transitive and intransitive: a recap

(i)   Remember that a transitive verb is one that takes a direct object in the accusative case; an intransitive one does not. Thus the Latin verb *dō* is transitive; without a direct object, it makes little or no sense. One cannot really just *give*; one needs to give *something*.

e.g.   *rēx dōnum dedit* = 'the king gave a gift.'

The Latin verb *ambulō*, by contrast, is intransitive; it *cannot* be followed by an object.

e.g.   *rēx ambulābat* = 'the king was walking.'

(ii)   Intransitive verbs are often followed by prepositions.

e.g.   *rēx cum amīcō ambulābat* = 'the king was walking *with* a friend.'

        rēx in agrō ambulābat = 'the king was walking *in* the field.'

(iii)   Some verbs, though, may be transitive or intransitive, according to the context.

e.g.   *in templum inībam* (intransitive; note use of preposition) = 'I was going *into* the temple.'
        templum inībam (transitive; note direct object in accusative) = 'I was entering the temple.'

e.g.   *in urbem trānsībam* (intransitive; note use of preposition) = 'I was crossing *into* the city.'
        flūmen trānsībam (transitive; note direct object in accusative) = 'I was crossing the river.'

Exercise 9.2

Write out in full the present and imperfect tenses, complete with meanings, of:

1.   *exeō*
2.   *ineō*
3.   *pereō*
4.   *redeō*
5.   *trānseō*

Exercise 9.3

Translate into English:

1. *cīvēs celeriter ex oppidō exībant.*
2. *omnēs in agrum inībātis.*
3. *puerī et puellae ab īnsulā redeunt.*
4. *quis herī circum templum ībat?*
5. *num servī flūmen sine dominō trānsībant?*
6. *ō iuvenis, nōnne mēcum Rōmam īs?*
7. *in magnō bellō multī hominēs pereunt.*
8. *ego et Sextus in oppidum trānsīmus.*
9. *parentēs nostrī tandem ad nōs redeunt.*
10. *dux vester proelium inībat.*

Exercise 9.4

Translate into Latin:

1. My friends are returning to Rome with me.
2. All the boys were going into the temple.
3. They are going around the town.
4. We often cross the river.
5. You (plur.) were perishing on the mountain.
6. You were going out of the fields, Aulus, weren't you?
7. Surely the soldiers were not returning to the city without their general, were they?
8. I am going to the fields now, and I shall work there.
9. Marcus often used to cross to the large island.
10. Many citizens are entering the battle.

More on nam, igitur and itaque

Let's squeeze in a little thing on *nam* here. We've met this word before, but we haven't really said much about it. Like our 'for', it is used to explain the reason for what has just been mentioned, and it comes at the beginning of its sentence.

e.g. *hodiē Rōmam it; nam mātrem suam vidēre cupit =*
      'He is going to Rome today; for he wishes to see his mother.'

On the other hand, *igitur* (= 'therefore') and *itaque* (= 'and so') are used to express the result of what has just been mentioned.

e.g. *ille aurum invēnit; laetus igitur est =*
      'He has found the gold; therefore he is happy.'

N.B. Remember not to put *igitur* first word in the sentence.

Latin likes to use words which bring out as clearly as possible the logical development of a passage, and sees no virtue, as we often do, in leaving things to the imagination.

Let us now return to the Roman Empire.

Exercise 9.5

Read the following passage carefully, and anwer the questions on it.

The Roman Empire: mad

<table>
<tr><td>

1

5

10
</td><td>

Caligula, ubi īrātus erat, dīxit ōlim: 'Rōma omnis ūnam
<u>cervīcem</u> habēre <u>dēbuit</u>.' nam eam omnem ūnō vulnere
<u>dētruncāre</u> cupīvit. multōs hominēs servōs suōs
occīdere iussit; multōs crūdēlissimē pūnīvit. ōlim mīlitēs
in <u>Galliam</u> ad mare mīsit. dīxērunt hominēs 'nunc
<u>Britanniam</u> occupābit.' nam Iūlius Caesar <u>Britanniam</u>
Rōmānīs ostenderat; nōn tamen occupāvit. sed mox
Caligula mīlitēs illōs nōn <u>victōriam</u> sed <u>conchās</u>
<u>reportāre</u> iussit. equum suum, nōmine Incitātum,
<u>cōnsulem</u> facere cōnstituit. mox Caligulam mīles,
nōmine Cassius Chaerea, necāvit. Caligulam Suētōnius,
<u>quī</u> <u>vītam</u> eius <u>dēscrīpsit</u>, <u>mōnstrum</u> vocāvit.
</td></tr>
</table>

cervīx, -īcis, f. = neck
dēbeō, -ēre, -uī, -itum (+ infin.)
  = I ought, must
dētruncō, -āre, -āvī, -ātum
  (here) = I behead
Gallia, -ae, f. = Gaul (roughly
  modern-day France)
Britannia, -ae, f. = Britain
victōria, -ae, f. = victory
concha, -ae, f. (here) = sea-shell
reportō, -āre, -āvī, -ātum =
  I bring back
cōnsul, -is, m. = consul
quī = who
vīta, -ae, f. = life
dēscrībō, -ere, dēscrīpsī,
  dēscrīptum = I write about
mōnstrum, -ī, n. (here) = monster

Notes:

(i) Suetonius (c. 69-140 A.D.) wrote the lives of Twelve Caesars (from Julius Caesar to Domitian).

(ii) The consuls were the highest ranking magistrates in the Republic (i.e. until the time of Augustus); two of them held office for one year, and it was rare for anyone to be consul more than once. In the Empire (i.e. from the time of Augustus onwards), the office was far less important, but it still commanded traditional respect and had some significance in the administration.

(iii) The Roman historian Tacitus (c. 55-115 A.D.) tells us that Julius Caesar could only be said to have 'shown Britain to the world, not to have handed it over'. The effective conquest of Britain was initiated about a century later than Caesar's efforts by the emperor Claudius, in 60 A.D. We learn a lot about it from Tacitus' life of his father-in-law, Agricola, who governed Britain from c.78 – 85 A.D. Incidentally, Tacitus is a wonderful writer and I recommend a reading of all his historical works (in translation – for the moment!).

1.   Answer the following questions:

(a) In lines 1-3, why did Caligula think that the whole of Rome ought to have had one neck?
(b) *multōs...iussit* (lines 3-4): this is a good example of Latin being ambiguous. Can you explain how this is so, and how our old friend, common sense, helps us to deal with this?
(c) In lines 4-6, for what reason did people think Caligula sent soldiers to Gaul?
(d) In lines 6-7, what was the extent of Julius Caesar's activities in Britain?
(e) In lines 9-10, what light does this bizarre proposal throw on Caligula's attitude to the consuls?
(f) In lines 10-11, what happened to Caligula in the end?
(g) In lines 11-12, what was Suetonius' opinion of Caligula?

2.   Translate the passage madly, but not too madly.

3.   Answer the following questions:

(a) In line 1, what would *ūnam* become in the genitive?
(b) In line 2, what case of what noun is *vulnere*?
(c) In line 4, what part of speech is *crūdēlissimē*?
(d) In line 5, what case is *Galliam* and why is it in this case?
(e) *iussit* (line 9): if, instead of 'he ordered', we wanted to say 'he will order', to what would we change *iussit*?
(f) In line 9, which word tells us whose horse Incitatus was?
(g) In line 10, what part of which verb is *facere*? Mention and translate any other examples of this form in the passage.

sē

We come now to another little word with a big meaning: the word is *sē*, and it is a reflexive pronoun. You will have dealt with reflexive pronouns in your French lessons when you met expressions such as *il s'appelle* (= 'he calls himself') or *il se lave* (= 'he washes himself'). Latin reflexive pronouns work in exactly the same way; in other words they mean 'himself', 'herself', 'itself' or 'themselves' and they 'reflect' the nominative that is governing the verb.

e.g.   'Cleopatra killed herself' = *Cleopatra sē necāvit.*
'Narcissus loved himself' = *Narcissus sē amābat.*
'The citizens were defending themselves' = *cīvēs sē dēfendēbant.*

They do not have a nominative (or vocative), and there is no difference between their singular and plural forms (hooray). This, then, is how *sē* goes:

Accusative	*sē*	himself, herself, itself, themselves
Genitive	*suī*	of himself, herself, itself, themselves
Dative	*sibi*	to or for himself, herself, itself, themselves
Ablative	*sē*	by, with or from himself, herself, itself, themselves

Note:
(i)   The final '*i*' of *sibi* can be long or short.
(ii)   The genitive *suī* is very rare, and we shall not be using it.
(iii)   As 'with you' = *tēcum*, so 'with himself' etc. is *sēcum.*

To show how *sē* may be used in the dative and ablative, here are a few more examples:
Dative: 'Lucius gave himself gifts' = *Lūcius sibi dōna dedit.*
Ablative: 'Lucius took books with him(self)'* = *Lūcius sēcum librōs portāvit.*

*Note that in English the 'self' is often left out, especially when the meaning is clear.

A final point or two on reflexives:

(iv) *sē*, being such a small word, can, if it wants to, double itself magically in the accusative and in the ablative, thus becoming *sēsē*. This is particularly useful in poetry if an extra syllable is required.

e.g. *Narcissus sēsē amāvit = Narcissus sē amāvit.*

(v) Finally, beware! 'Himself' etc. (in English) can be dative as well as accusative.

e.g. 'This master gave (to) himself a good slave' =
*hic dominus **sibi** bonum servum dedit.*

Not to be mixed up with:
'This slave gave himself to a good master' =
*hic servus **sē** bonō dominō dedit.*

So much for reflexives.

Exercise 9.6

Translate into English:

1. *hī iuvenēs sē semper laudant.*
2. *cīvēs illī sē celeriter ā proeliō mōvērunt.*
3. *hic puer forte sē gladiō vulnerāvit.*
4. *Mārcus sibi verba poētae nārrābat.*
5. *dux ille, ubi hostēs eum vīcērunt, sē occīdit.*
6. *sibi crās aurum nōn dabunt.*
7. *nōnne sē ā malō dominō līberābit?*
8. *Narcissus sē in aquā cōnspexit.*
9. *Aulus, quamquam fessus erat, sē fortiter dēfendit.*
10. *quid sēcum senex ille portāvit?*

Exercise 9.7

Translate into Latin:

1. Narcissus loved himself.
2. These soldiers have given themselves new swords.
3. This old man has carried many books with him(self) to the city.
4. Gaius and Sextus will always praise themselves.
5. Why is Narcissus watching himself in the river?
6. The girls are saying to themselves the words of the poet.
7. He saw himself yesterday in the water.
8. The sad general has handed himself over to the enemy.
9. This old man sings to himself when is he working.
10. Yesterday this little boy wounded himself by chance.

N.B. *sē gerit* ... + an adverb = 'he behaves himself *in a certain way*.'
e.g. *sē bene gerunt* = 'they behave themselves well.'

eō: more tenses

But now it's time to return to *eō* and its compounds. So far, we've had the present and the imperfect tenses. Let us turn now to the future and the perfect.

Future tense

1st person singular	*ībō*	I shall go
2nd person singular	*ībis*	you (sing.) will go
3rd person singular	*ībit*	he, she, it will go
1st person plural	*ībimus*	we shall go
2nd person plural	*ībitis*	you (pl.) will go
3rd person plural	*ībunt*	they will go

This behaves itself well. It is completely consistent with itself, and presents us with no difficulty. In fact, let's face it, it would have been nice if *audiō* had gone like this!

Perfect tense

1st person singular	*iī*	I have gone, went
2nd person singular	*īstī*	you (sing.) have gone, went
3rd person singular	*iit*	he, she, it has gone, went
1st person plural	*iimus*	we have gone, went
2nd person plural	*īstis*	you (pl.) have gone, went
3rd person plural	*iērunt*	they have gone, went

Notes:
(i) The 2nd persons singular and plural of the perfect tense contract to *īstī* and *īstis,* although in compounds, the forms '-*iistī*' and '-*iistis*' are also found.

(ii) Perfect tense forms with a '*v*' (e.g. *īvī, īvistī, īvit* etc.) are also found, both in the simple verb and in its compounds; but these are rarer and in the perfect of the very common compound verb *redeō* are not found at all.

(iii) The pluperfect is completely regular; it is *ieram, ierās, ierat* etc. in the simple verb and (for example) *exieram, exierās, exierat* etc. in the compounds.

Three final things (for the moment) about *eō*:

(i) the present infinitive of *eō* is *īre* = 'to go';
(ii) the singular imperative (2nd person) is simply *ī* = 'go!'
(iii) the plural imperative (2nd person) is *īte* = 'go!'

Exercise 9.8

Write out in full the future and perfect tenses, complete with meanings, of:

1. *exeō*
2. *ineō*
3. *pereō*

4. *redeō*
5. *trānseō*

Exercise 9.9

Translate into English:

1. *mox in agrōs trānsībimus.*
2. *tandem in hoc oppidum inīstis.*
3. *rediitne ille senex ad īnsulam?*
4. *hīc flūmen trānsībō.* (Be careful!)
5. *multī cīvēs subitō ex urbe exiērunt.*
6. *puerī et puellae templum inībunt.*
7. *fortēs mīlitēs in proeliō perierant.*
8. *crās omnēs in agrōs redībimus.*
9. *num mulierēs circum montem ībunt?*
10. *nōnne omnēs equī ex agrō exībunt?*

Exercise 9.10

Translate into Latin:

1. Tomorrow we shall enter the temple.
2. Yesterday the soldiers went out of the city.
3. The boys and girls crossed into the fields.
4. Aulus and I have gone into the town.
5. The youths had returned to the river.
6. The women crossed the road as quickly as possible.
7. Will they really go out of the temple tomorrow?
8. Laelia, did you go to the mountain?
9. Sulpicia and I went around the field.
10. Surely you returned yesterday, Marcus, didn't you?

autem

Before proceeding to our next story, we might as well squeeze in a few words about *autem*.
autem very often means 'however' or 'but', and like *tamen*, does not come first word in its sentence. The word *autem* also often brings in something additional which is not contrasted with what has gone before. The words 'but' and 'however' in English always introduce a contrast; so does *tamen* in Latin; but *autem* can be used just to carry the story along, in which case it is often best translated simply by 'moreover' or 'and'.

Let us now turn to Caligula's successor, before we leave the Roman Empire for the time being.
A great deal of our knowledge of Claudius comes from the Roman historian Tacitus; a lot too comes from Suetonius. Claudius was called by his own mother, Antonia, 'a freak…of a man, not completed by Nature, but only begun.' If ever she accused anyone of stupidity, she would call the person even more stupid than her son Claudius. We are also told how he was despised and derided by the rest of his family. It was never remotely envisaged that he would ever be Emperor. Indeed, if inferiority complexes had been thought of in his day, he ought to have had one the size of Mount Everest! Instead, on becoming Emperor at the age of fifty, he took to the job like a duck to water and on the whole made a considerable success of it.

Incidentally, I have rather uncritically implied that the successful invasion of Britain was 'a good thing'. This is certainly what the Romans thought, and it is generally assumed that we think likewise.

Exercise 9.11

Read the following passage carefully and answer the questions on it.

The Roman Empire: from mad to not so bad

1   *post Caligulam fuit Claudius, <u>patruus</u> eius. hunc, <u>quī</u>*
     <u>dēfōrmis</u> erat et <u>portentōsus</u>, <u>cognātī</u> eius <u>vel</u>
     <u>neglēxērunt vel irrīsērunt</u>. iam <u>senior</u>, ubi Caligulam
     occīdit Chaerea sē in <u>Palātiō</u> perterritus inter <u>vēla</u>
5   *<u>abdidit</u>; <u>pedēs</u> autem eius mīles, <u>quī</u> cum comitibus in*
     <u>Palātium</u> ruerat, cōnspexit; et eum ad <u>castra</u> mīlitum
     dūxit. ibi eum mīlitēs nōn, <u>ut</u> timuerat, occīdērunt, sed in
     nōmen eius <u>iūrāvērunt</u>; sīc Claudius <u>prīnceps</u> fuit. is,
     quamquam <u>noxiōs</u> <u>crūdēliter</u> pūniēbat, sē saepe
10   *<u>sapienter</u> gerēbat; multa bene fēcit. Claudius prīmus*
     Rōmānōrum Britanniae magnam partem <u>imperiō</u>
     Rōmānō <u>addidit</u>. eum tandem quārta uxor Agrippīna,
     <u>quae</u> iam māter fuit <u>Nerōnis</u>, <u>fortasse</u>, auxiliō <u>bōlētī</u>,
     occīdit; et post eum <u>prīnceps</u> fuit <u>Nerō</u>.

patruus, -ī, m. = paternal uncle
quī, m. = who
dēfōrmis, -e (here) = ugly
portentōsus, -a, -um (here) = freakish
cognātus, -ī, m. = a relative
vel...vel = either...or
neglegō, -ere, -ēxi, -ēctum = I neglect
irrīdeō, -ēre, irrīsī, irrīsum (+ acc.) = I make fun of
senior, -is, m. (here) = middle-aged
Palātium, -ī, n. = the Palace
vēlum, -ī, n. (here) = curtain
abdō, -ere, -didī, -ditum = I hide (trans.)
pēs, pedis, m. = foot
castra, -ōrum, n. pl. = camp
ut (here) = as
in nōmen iūrō, -āre (+ gen.) = I swear allegiance to
prīnceps, -ipis, m. (here) = Emperor
noxius, -a, -um = guilty
crūdēliter = cruelly
sapienter = wisely
imperium, -iī, n. (here) = Empire
addō, -ere, -didī, -ditum = I add
fortasse = perhaps
quae, f. = who
Nerō, Nerōnis, m. = Nero
bōlētus, -ī, m. = mushroom

1.   Answer the following questions:

(a) In lines 1-3, what made Claudius' family assess him so wrongly?
(b) In lines 4-6, where did Claudius hide and how was he discovered?
(c) In line 7, what did Claudius think was going to happen to him?
(d) In lines 7-8, what happened to him instead?
(e) In lines 9-12, why do you think that Claudius was considered to have been a successful ruler?
(f) What do lines 12-14 tell us about Claudius' married life?
(g) And what do they tell us about Agrippina?
(h) In line 14, what happened after the death of Claudius?

2.   Translate the passage portentously.

3.   Answer the following questions:

(a) *occīdit* (line 4): put this verb into the future tense.
(b) In lines 5-6, had the soldier rushed into the Palace alone? Explain your answer.
(c) In line 6, what is the tense of *ruerat*?
(d) *nōmen* (line 8): put this noun into the plural and translate it.
(e) In line 8, what is the case of *eius*, and to whom does it refer?
(f) *quamquam...pūniēbat* (line 9): discuss the position of these words in the sentence.
(g) In line 9, what part of speech is *sē*?
(h) In line 14, if, instead of 'Nero was Emperor', we wanted to say 'Nero will be Emperor', what would we have to write instead of *fuit*?

So now, make sure you order your Book 3 well in advance, to hear all the latest about the one-and-only Nero, who, among other things, is said to have fiddled while Rome burnt (except that they didn't have fiddles then!)

Numbers: 11-20

And here is something which we've totally forgotten about. (Incidentally – dare I say this? – I don't see anything terribly wrong in ending a sentence with a preposition, as I did just then.) However, with apologies for that digression, remember our adventure into the higher mysteries of mathematics, which took us as far as the number 10? Well, now we're going to show you that we can go twice as far, if we really try. So here goes:

Numerals 11-20

XI	*ūndecim*
XII	*duodecim*
XIII	*tredecim*
XIV	*quattuordecim*
XV	*quīndecim*
XVI	*sēdecim*
XVII	*septendecim*
XVIII	*duodēvīgintī*
XIX	*ūndēvīgintī*
XX	*vīgintī*

Notes:
(i)   By putting an X on the left of the simple numerals, we have added ten to them, thus producing eleven to twenty. Magic, eh?

(ii)   All these numbers, including *vīgintī,* are delightfully indeclinable; there is no need to try to put them into any other case, or to make them 'agree'. Thus, 'I saw twenty girls' would be *vīgintī puellās vīdī.*

(iii) *duodēvīgintī* means, literally, 'two down from twenty', hence 'eighteen'. *ūndēvīgintī* means, literally, 'one down from twenty', hence 'nineteen'. Brilliant, eh? Who said the Romans weren't all that hot at maths?

Exercise 9.12

Translate into English:

1.   *hoc tredecim puellae fēcērunt.*
2.   *duodecim puerī cum sex iuvenibus pugnābant.*
3.   *Quīntus ūndecim librōs scrīpsit.*
4.   *Lūcius quattuordecim servōrum dominus est.*
5.   *vīgintī puellīs vīgintī librōs dedī.*
6.   *ūndēvīgintī mīlitēs oppidum iniērunt.*
7.   *in hōc oppidō septendecim magnae viae sunt.*
8.   *quīndecim equī in hīs agrīs stant.*
9.   *duodēvīgintī hominēs in templō cantant.*
10. *cīvēs sēdecim hōs mūrōs aedificāvērunt.*

Exercise 9.13

Translate the following sums into Latin words, using *et* for + and *sunt* for =.

1.   XVI + III = XIX
2.   X + X = XX
3.   XV + II = XVII
4.   XI + VII = XVIII
5.   XII + II = XIV
6.   XIII + IV = XVII

I hope I've got these right!

Exercise 9.14

Translate into Latin:

1.   There are eleven boys in that road.
2.   Twelve women were going around the temple.
3.   Can't you see those fifteen old men, Sulpicia?
4.   Many soldiers were fighting with nineteen citizens.
5.   Six brave youths overcame the seventeen sailors.
6.   These leaders attacked thirteen cities.
7.   Fourteen farmers are working in their fields.
8.   Sixteen inhabitants were making a long journey.
9.   Manius, can you really hear all eighteen girls?
10. I approached the mountain with twenty companions.

Exercise 9.15

Match up the Latin words (1-5) with the English words (a-e). Explain the connexion between the English and the Latin words.

1.	*exeō*	(a)	exit
2.	*pereō*	(b)	transit
3.	*trānseō*	(c)	dormitory
4.	*dormiō*	(d)	perish

Exercise 9.16

Translate into Latin:

1. The good master was praising the tired slaves.
2. The strong inhabitants were building a big wall.
3. The happy maid-servants love the new queen.
4. The angry teachers were warning the bad boys.
5. Wretched women fear long wars.
6. Moreover, many soldiers rushed into the town.
7. The leaders led their forces with them into the city.
8. The old men were frightened because of the king's anger.
9. My friend will go to Rome with me.
10. The brave youths said many things on behalf of the little girls.

plūs and plūrimus

Remember the one vicious comparison which we have not mentioned yet? Perhaps you were hoping we had forgotten about it? Well we hadn't! We were waiting until you were old enough to take it in your stride. And here it is – or as you will find out as you read on, here it isn't:

multus	*(plūs)*	*plūrimus*
much	more	very many

1. So then; we seem to have now met the comparative of *multus* (= much). But here comes the big shock; *multus* does not actually have a comparative in the singular. Instead, we have to make do with the neuter singular noun *plūs* (= more), and use it in the same way that we use 'more of' in English: e.g. 'I want more of the pudding' (rather than simply 'I want more pudding'). It goes as follows:

Nominative	*plūs*
Vocative	*plūs*
Accusative	*plūs*
Genitive	*plūris*
Dative*	–
Ablative	*plūre*

* N.B. The dative singular does not appear to exist – so feel free not to use it!

And this is how we use *plūs*. Be sure to note that, in the singular, in Latin, we use a genitive case after it.

e.g.   'I desire more money' = *plūs pecūniae cupiō*.
           'He has more gold than courage' = *plūs aurī habet quam virtūtis*.

In the plural however, to make this easier, we have *plūrēs*, which is a 3rd declension adjective and goes as follows:

	Masculine	**Feminine**	**Neuter**
Nominative	*plūrēs*	*plūrēs*	*plūra*
Vocative	*plūrēs*	*plūrēs*	*plūra*
Accusative	*plūrēs*	*plūrēs*	*plūra*
Genitive	*plūrium*	*plūrium*	*plūrium*
Dative	*plūribus*	*plūribus*	*plūribus*
Ablative	*plūribus*	*plūribus*	*plūribus*

Note that the neuter plural ends in *-a*, not *-ia*.

e.g.   'He has more friends than I do' = *plūrēs amīcōs habet quam ego*.
           'I wish to say more words' = *plūra verba dīcere cupiō*.
           'He is the leader of more soldiers' = *dux plūrium mīlitum est*.

2.   After the initial shock of the comparative, the superlative of *multus* causes no difficulty, beyond the fact that, as with the comparative *plūs*, it bears no obvious relation to the word *multus* and just has to be learnt. It is *plūrimus, -a, -um* (= 'most' or 'very many') and goes like *bonus*. That, at least, is a relief.

e.g.   'Very many soldiers were fighting' = *plūrimī mīlitēs pugnābant*.
           'We saw very many inhabitants' = *plūrimōs incolās vīdimus*.

Exercise 9.17

Translate into English:

1.   *ille plus habet aurī quam rēx.*
2.   *quis plūrēs librōs habet quam ille?*
3.   *hastās plūribus puerīs quam iuvenibus dedī.*
4.   *plūrēs incolae plūs pecūniae habent.*
5.   *ille agricola plūs vīnī quam hic bibit.*
6.   *plūrimī cīvēs bella nōn amant.*
7.   *ille dux cum plūrimīs comitibus urbem iniit.*
8.   *senēs plūra quam iuvenēs dīxērunt.*

Exercise 9.18

Translate into Latin:

1. I shall say more words to you (pl.) tomorrow.
2. Give us more food, Sulpicia.
3. There is more anger than courage in that man.
4. Marcus has more gold than Aulus.
5. This farmer has very many horses.
6. This land has more cities than that one.
7. I shall give very many books to the wise girls.
8. Most inhabitants desire more money.

Vocabulary 9

Vocabulary 9

ūndecim = eleven
duodecim = twelve
tredecim = thirteen
quattuordecim = fourteen
quīndecim = fifteen
sēdecim = sixteen
septendecim = seventeen
duodēvīgintī = eighteen
ūndēvīgintī = nineteen
vīgintī = twenty
prō + abl. = on behalf of, in front of
sine + abl. = without
sub + abl. = under
sē = himself, herself, itself, themselves

So here we are again, hovering on the brink of our last chapter: and it seems as if we had only just started this book. Ah well! let us at least tackle the following stories brilliantly!

Chapter 10

Exam practice

As in Chapter 10 of Book 1, we are presenting you now with three beautiful stories in the format set in the Common Entrance exam; so you will know exactly what to expect.

Exercise 10.1

Read the following passage (do not write a translation) and answer the questions below in English. Complete sentences are not required.

Orpheus, the wonderful singer of songs, loses his wife, Eurydice

1   Orpheus, fīlius Calliopēae _prīmae_ _Mūsārum_, in Thrāciā
     habitābat; is ubi cantābat, nōn _sōlum_ hominēs sed etiam
     ferae circum eum stābant, flūmina _nōn iam_ _fluēbant,_
     montēs et _arborēs_ eī appropinquābant; nam omnēs et
5   omnia eum audīre cupiēbant. uxor eius, nōmine Eurydicē,
     nympha erat pulcherrima et _dulcissima;_ hanc ille
     magnopere amāvit et illum haec; laetissimī erant et ille et
     haec; sed hanc _serpēns_ _momordit_ et occīdit; eius morte
     Orpheus miserrimus erat; ex _Tartarō_ eam in _orbem_
10   _terrārum_ redūcere magnopere cupīvit. locum igitur illum
     saevum et trīstem inīre fortissimē cōnstituit.

prīma (here) = foremost
Mūsa, -ae, f. = Muse
sōlum (adverb) = only
fera, -ae, f. = wild beast
nōn iam = no longer
fluō, -ere, flūxī, flūxum = I flow
arbor, arboris, f. = tree
nympha, -ae, f. = nymph
dulcis, -e = sweet
serpēns, -entis, c. = snake
mordeō, -ēre, momordī,
morsum = I bite
Tartarus, -ī, m. = the Underworld
orbis terrārum = the circle of
lands, the world

1.   (a) In line 1, who was Orpheus?
     (b   In lines 2-4, what happened when Orpheus sang?
     (c) In lines 5-6, whom did Orpheus marry? Describe her.
     (d) In line 8, what event brought Orpheus' happiness to an end?
     (e) In lines 8-9, what was Orpheus' mood after the fatal snake-bite?
     (f) In lines 9-10, what did Orpheus want to do?
     (g) In lines 10-11, what did Orpheus decide to do?
     (h) In lines 10-11, how is the Underworld described?

Notes:

(i)   _Mūsārum_ (line 1): There were nine Muses: they were goddesses of poetry, music and other arts.

(ii)   _Thrācia_ (line 1) = 'Thrace', a large region to the North of Greece. There Diomedes lived (remember?) until he was gobbled up by his mares (see Book 1, Chapter 3).

(iii)   _Eurydicē_ (line 5): in English we pronounce 'c' as 's' before 'e', 'i', 'y' and 'ae': e.g. _Caesar._ But remember, in classical Latin, the 'c' is always hard like 'k'.

(iv)   _nympha_ (line 6): The nymphs were young female spirits of natural features such as mountains, trees and rivers, and also of cities, places and states. Although they were daughters of Jupiter, they were mortal. They were generally beautiful and were lovers of the arts.

(v)   _morte_ (line 9): note that the ablative often means 'at'.

Exercise 10.2

Translate the following passage into good English:

Orpheus charms the Underworld

1   *Orpheus, ubi in <u>Tartarum</u> advēnit, etiam ibi omnēs
    <u>carminibus</u> suīs superāvit; nōn <u>sōlum</u> <u>Charōnem</u>, <u>quī</u> in
    <u>lintre</u> suā mortuōs in <u>Tartarum</u> <u>vehēbat</u>, sed etiam
    Cerberum, <u>canem</u> saevissimum, <u>quī</u> <u>tria</u> <u>capita</u> habēbat,*
5   *<u>mollīvit</u>; omnēs autem mortuī et omnia <u>mōnstra</u> et
    <u>portenta</u> <u>nōn iam</u>, ubi Orpheus cantābat, <u>fremēbant</u>, sed
    laetī et <u>quiētī</u> eum audiēbant. tandem rēx <u>Tartarī</u>, Plūtō,
    et rēgīna, Prōserpina, haec verba eī dīxērunt: '<u>licet</u> tibi
    uxōrem tuam ex <u>tenebrīs</u> <u>Tartarī</u> in <u>orbem terrārum</u>*
10 *redūcere; tū prīmus ī, et haec post tē ībit; sed antequam
    haec in terrā erit, nōlī eām <u>respicere</u>: <u>sī</u> id faciēs,
    numquam eam vīvam iterum vidēbis.'*

Tartarus, -ī, m. = the Underworld
carmen, -inis, n. = song
sōlum (adverb) = only
Charōn, -ōnis, m. = Charon
quī = who
linter, lintris, f. = boat
vehō, -ere, vēxī, vectum =
    I convey
canis, -is, c. = dog
tria (n. of *trēs*) = three
caput, capitis, n. = head
molliō, -īre, -īvī, -ītum = I soften
mōnstrum, -ī, n. (here) =
    monster
portentum, -ī, n. (here) = freak
nōn iam = no longer
fremō, -ere, fremuī, fremitum =
    I howl
quiētus, -a, -um = quiet
licet + dat. = it is permitted
tenebrae, -ārum, f. pl. =
    darkness
orbis terrārum = the world
respiciō, -ere, respexī,
    respectum = I look back at
sī = if

Exercise 10.3

Study the following passage and answer the questions below in good English. Complete sentences are not required.

Orpheus' joy, alas! is short-lived

1 *laetissimus, Orpheus ex <u>Tartarō</u> exībat; et post eum*	Tartarus, -ī, m. = the Underworld
laetissima ībat Eurydicē; et iam ille in <u>orbem terrārum</u>	orbis terrārum = the world
redierat, et iam post eum lūcī appropinquābat Eurydicē.	quod (here) = which
sed Orpheus id <u>quod</u> iusserant Plūtō et Prōserpina	ēheu! = alas!
5 *facere nōn potuit; et <u>ēheu</u>! ubi Eurydicē <u>nōndum</u> in <u>orbe</u>*	nōndum = not yet
<u>terrārum</u> fuit, <u>respexit</u>! statim illa <u>nōn iam</u> <u>appāruit</u>. tum	nōn iam = no longer
Orpheus per terrās miserrimus errābat et <u>carmina</u>	respiciō, -ere, respexī,
trīstissima cantābat. eum tandem mulierēs, <u>quae</u> deum	respectum = I look back at
Bacchum <u>colēbant</u>, quod Apollinem Bacchō <u>praeferēbat</u>,	appāreō, -ēre, -uī, -itum (here) =
10 *occīdērunt; et caput eius illae in flūmen Hebrum*	I am visible
iēcērunt; et flūmen ad mare caput portāvit et undae ad	carmen, -inis, n. = song
Lesbum īnsulam <u>vēxērunt</u>; et semper <u>carmen</u> trīste sed	quae, f. = who
pulchrum cantābat.	colō, -ere, coluī, cultum (here) =
	I worship
	praeferō (very irregular) =
	I prefer
	vehō, -ere, vēxī, vectum =
	I convey

(a) In line 3, what is the tense of *redierat*? What does it come from and what does it mean?

(b) *lūcī* (line 3): what case of what noun is this?

(c) In line 5, what would *nōn potuit* become in the imperfect?

(d) In line 6, what is the neuter of *illa*?

(e) In line 7, what is the case of *carmina*? Why is it in this case?

(f) *iēcērunt* (line 11): Give the principal parts and meaning of this verb.

(g) *ad Lesbum* (lines 11-12): what do we learn about this island from these words?

(h) In line 13, if, instead of 'it was singing' we wanted to say 'it will sing', what change should we make to *cantābat*?

Notes.

(i) *Bacchus, -ī*, m. (line 9), was the god of wine and revelry.

(ii) *Apollo, Apollinis*, m. (line 9), was the god of light, music and prophecy among other things.

(iii) The *Hebrus* (line 10) was a river in Thrace.

(iv) We regularly know Lesbus (line 12) by its Greek name Lesbos.

Exercise 10.4

Using the vocabulary given below, translate into Latin:

(i) The good queen was praising the tired maid-servants.

good = *bonus, -a, -um;* queen = *rēgīna, -ae*, f.; I praise = *laudō* (1); tired = *fessus, -a, -um*; maid-servant = *ancilla, -ae*, f.

(ii) The small boys fear a long war.

small = *parvus, -a, -um;* boy = *puer, -ī*, m.; I fear = *timeō* (2); long = *longus, -a, -um;* war = *bellum, -ī*, n.

Exercise 10.5

Study the following passage (do not write a translation) and answer the questions below in English. Complete sentences are not required.

Bellerophon the suppliant

1   *Bellerophōn, iuvenis, Corinthum habitābat; sed ubi et*
     frātrem suum et alium cīvem occīdit, Tīrynthem supplex
     fūgit ad rēgem Proetum; huius uxor, ubi iuvenem vīdit,
     eum statim amāvit, sed, ubi eam sprēvit, īrātissima
5   *coniugī suō dīxit 'Bellerophōn mē sibi habēre cupit;*
     occīde eum.' sed Proetus eum, quod supplex erat, ipse
     occīdere nōn potuit; iussit igitur eum ad patrem uxōris,
     rēgem Lyciae, quī nōmine Īobatēs erat, epistolam
     portāre obsignātam; in eā epistolā haec verba scrīpsit:
10   *'eum quī hanc tibi epistolam dabit occīde; nam uxōrem*
     meam, tuam fīliam, sibi habēre cōnstituit.' Īobatēs
     quoque hospitem ipse necāre nōn cupīvit; dīxit igitur
     Bellerophontī: 'hoc tē rogō; laetum mē fac; Chimaeram
     dēlē.' Chimaera mōnstrum erat ingentissimum et
15   *saevissimum.*

Bellerophōn, -ontis, m. = Bellerophon
Corinthus, -ī, f. = Corinth
alius, -a, -ud (irregular) = other
Tīrȳns, Tīrynthis, f. = Tiryns
supplex, -icis (adj. & noun) = suppliant
sperno, -ere, sprēvī, sprētum = I despise, reject
ipse (here) = himself
epistola, -ae, f. = letter
obsignātus, -a, -um = sealed
quī = who
hospes, -itis, c. = guest (or host)
Chimaera, -ae, f. = the Chimaera
mōnstrum, -ī, n. (here) = monster

(a) In lines 1-3, why did Bellerophon flee from Corinth?
(b) In lines 3-5, why did Proteus' wife not tell her husband the truth about Bellerophon?
(c) In lines 6-7, how did Proetus react on being told by his wife to kill Bellerophon?
(d) In lines 7-8, what was Proetus' relationship to Iobates?
(e) In lines 7-11, describe Proetus' method of trying to remain innocent of killing Bellerophon?
(f) In lines 11-12, how did Iobates react to Proetus' letter?
(g) In lines 12-14, what did Iobates ask Bellerophon to do?
(h) In lines 14-15, who or what was the Chimaera?

Notes:
(i)   Corinth (line 1) was a very famous Greek city in the north of the Peloponnese, on the Corinthian gulf. Note that it is feminine. Although we tend to assume that 2nd declension nouns in *-us* are masculine, some are not. As a general rule, the names of most islands, countries, cities and trees are feminine.

(ii)   Tiryns (line 2) was a very ancient city near Argos and Mycenae in the North East of the Peloponnese. Lycia (line 8) was a country in Asia Minor.

(iii) A 'suppliant' person (line 6) was commonly one who fled as an outcast to a powerful ruler for protection. It was very wicked to kill a suppliant.

(iv)   A 'guest' (*hospes, -itis,* c.) (line 12) was also someone who depended on being protected by his host. According to the laws of hospitality, it was very wicked to kill him! So both Proetus and Iobates wanted to get Bellerophon killed without doing the dirty work themselves.

Exercise 10.6

Translate the following passage into good English:

Bellerophon victorious

1   *itaque Chimaeram Bellerophōn dēlēre cupīvit; ea trēs*
   partēs habuit: ūna pars <u>leaena</u> fuit, <u>alia</u> pars fuit <u>capra</u>,
   tertia <u>dracō</u>: illa <u>ignem</u> <u>spīrābat</u>. sed Minerva eī equum
   <u>ālātum</u> nōmine Pēgasum dedit; auxiliō Pēgasī,
5   *Bellerophōn super Chimaeram <u>volāvit</u> et eam multīs*
   sagittīs superāvit. Īobatēs tamen nōn <u>sōlum</u> <u>ingrātus</u>
   erat sed Bellerophontem multa <u>alia</u> perīcula inīre et aliōs
   multōs superāre iussit; et eōs omnēs auxiliō Pēgasī
   superāvit; tandem mīlitēs suōs Īobatēs iuvenem
10   *occīdere iussit; sed servāvit eum Neptūnus, <u>quī</u> in*
   <u>campum</u>, ubi rēgis <u>rēgia</u> stetit, undās mittēbat magnās.
   posteā dīxit Īobatēs Bellerophontī: 'id <u>quod</u> dē tē lēgī,
   <u>vērum</u> nōn est; <u>in</u> tē magnopere <u>peccāvī</u>: <u>ignōsce</u> mihi.'

leaena, -ae, f. = lioness
alius, -a, -ud (irregular) = other
capra, -ae, f. = she-goat
dracō, -ōnis, m. = dragon
ignis, -is, m. = fire
spīrō, -āre, -āvī, -ātum = I breathe
ālātus, -a, -um = winged
volō, -āre, -āvī, -ātum = I fly
sōlum (adverb) = only
ingrātus, -a, -um = ungrateful
quī = who
campus, -ī, m. = a plain
rēgia, -ae, f. = palace
quod (here) = which
vērus, -a, -um = true
in + acc. (here) = against
peccō, -āre, -āvī, -ātum = I sin
ignōscō, -ere, ignōvī, ignōtum
   (+ dat.) = I forgive

(i)   Minerva (line 3), known to the Greeks as Athena, was a very powerful virgin goddess of wisdom and the arts.

(ii)   Neptune (line 10), known to the Greeks as Poseidon, was very powerful as god of the sea. There was also a tradition that it was Neptune who gave Pegasus to Bellerophon.

Exercise 10.7

Study the following passage and answer the questions below in English. Complete sentences are not required.

Bellerophon, alas! brought low

1	*tum Īobatēs Bellerophontī <u>aliam</u> fīliam suam dedit*	*alius, -a, -ud* (irregular) = other
	uxōrem; ea nōmine erat Philonoē; et dīxit Īobatēs	*sē rēgāliter gerere* = to behave
	Bellerophontī 'tū post mē rēx eris Lyciae.' Bellerophōn	like a king
	tum <u>sē rēgāliter gerēbat</u> et laetissimus erat; sed ōlim ad	*volō, -āre, -āvī, -ātum* = I fly
5	*montem Olympum, auxiliō Pēgasī, <u>volāre</u> cōnstituit; nam*	*immortālis, -e* = immortal
	ibi dī <u>immortālēs</u> habitābant; et Bellerophōn iam sibi	*similis, -e* (+ dat. or gen.) =
	dīcēbat 'tū deō <u>immortālī</u> <u>similis</u> es.' Iuppiter igitur <u>asīlum</u>	similar
	Pēgasum sub <u>caudā</u> <u>pungere</u> iussit; is sē subitō <u>ērēxit</u> et	*asīlus, -ī,* m. = gadfly
	Bellerophontem ad terram iēcit. deinde Iuppiter Pēgasum	*cauda, -ae,* f. = tail
10	*cēpit et <u>fulmina</u> sua portāre iussit; Bellerophōn autem in*	*pungō, -ere, pupugī, pūnctum*
	<u>spīnās</u> <u>cecidit</u>; et hae eum magnopere vulnerāvērunt; et	= I sting
	posteā per terrās errābat sōlus, <u>nec</u> <u>aliōs</u> hominēs	*ērigō, -ere, ērēxī, ērēctum* =
	salūtāre cupiēbat; sīc dī eōs pūniēbant <u>quī</u> sibi dīcēbant	I raise
	'tū deō similis es.'	*fulmen, -inis,* n. = thunderbolt
		spīna, -ae, f. = thorn
		cadō, -ere, cecidī, cāsum =
		I fall
		nec = nor, and… not
		quī = who

Note:
Mount Olympus (line 5), right up in the North, was the highest peak in Greece and was regarded as the home of the gods.

(a) In line 1, put *dedit* into the imperfect.
(b) In line 5, what is the case of *auxiliō* and what does it come from?
(c) *dī* (line 6): what is the vocative singular of this word?
(d) In line 7, if, instead of 'he used to say', we had wished to write 'he will say', what would we have to write instead of *dīcēbat*?
(e) In line 10, give the principal parts of the verb from which *cēpit* comes.
(f) Mention and translate all the prepositions in the passage, together with the words they govern.
(g) In line 11, what is the tense of *vulnerāvērunt*? And how would you translate it here?
(h) In line 13, which part of which word is *eōs*?

Exercise 10.8

Using the vocabulary given below, translate into Latin:

(i)   We fear the strong sailors.
    timeō (2) = I fear; *validus, -a, -um* = strong; *nauta, -ae,* m. = sailor

(ii)   The little boys were watching the big horses.
    parvus, -a, -um = little; *puer, puerī,* m. = boy; *spectō* (1) = I watch; *magnus, -a, -um* = big;
    equus, -ī, m. = horse

Exercise 10.9

Study the following passage (do not write a translation) and answer the questions below in English. Complete sentences are not required.

Some adventures of Theseus when he was still a boy

1   *Aegeus et Aethra parentēs erant Thēseī; in urbe*
     Troezēne habitābant; sed mox Aegeus, quī rēx erat
     Athēnārum, Athēnās rediit; is antequam discessit,
     gladium suum et crepidās sub saxō relīquit et uxōrī suae
5   *dīxit: 'ubi puer saxum movēre poterit, id quod sub eō est*
     Athēnās illum portāre iubē.' ubi sēdecim annōs nātus
     est, Thēseus saxum mōvit et gladium et crepidās patris
     Athēnās portābat. prope Corinthum habitābat Sinis,
     homō saevissimus: is verticem arboris ad terram
10   *flectēbat et sī quis forte per agrōs iter faciēbat, ab illō*
     auxilium rogābat; tum ubi ille summam arborem
     tenēbat, eam subitō ēmittēbat: arbor quam celerrimē
     cum homine ad caelum ēvolābat: et illum ad terram
     iaciēbat et occīdēbat. Sinis Thēseum sīc necāre cupīvit,
15   *sed eum Thēseus ipse superāvit et occīdit.*

Troezēn, Troezēnis, f. = Troezen
quī = who
crepida, -ae, f = sandal
saxum, -ī, n. = rock
relinquō, -ere, relīquī, relictum
    = I leave
quod (here) = which
annōs nātus = years old
vertex, -icis, m. (here) = the top
arbor, -is, f. = tree
flectō, -ere, flexī, flexum =
    I bend
sī quis = if anyone
ēmittō, -ere, ēmīsī, ēmissum =
    I let go
ēvolō, -āre, -āvī, -ātum = I fly up
ipse = himself

(a) In lines 2-3, why was it appropriate for Aegeus to return to Athens?
(b) In line 5, what is referred to by *id quod sub eō est*?
(c) In lines 6-8, what did Theseus do when he was sixteen years old?
(d) In lines 8-9, who was Sinis and where did he live?
(e) In lines 10-11, whom did Sinis regularly ask to help him?
(f) In lines 11-14, how did Sinis dispose of his victims? Explain in full.
(g) Do you agree that Sinis must have been very strong. Give a reason for your answer.
(h) In lines 14-15, what happened to Sinis in the end?

Notes:

(i)   *Athēnae, -ārum,* f. (line 3) is the Latin for Athens. Note that it is a plural name.

       The journey to Athens from Troezen, an ancient city in the north-east of the Peloponnese (southern Greece), of which Pittheus, Theseus' maternal grandfather, was king, would go through Corinth and Megara.

(ii)   *Corinthus, -ī,* f. (line 8) is so well-known that we call it Corinth. (Like most cities in the singular, it is feminine.) It is just south of the Corinthian gulf, which divides Greece in two.

(iii) While we're at it, let's note that *arbor, -is* = 'tree' is feminine and that most trees are feminine.

       e.g.*ulmus, -ī,* f. = 'elm'; *salix, salicis,* f. = 'willow'

       Most islands, also, are feminine.

Exercise 10.10

Translate the following passage into good English:

Sciron and Procrustes

1 *iam appropinquābat Thēseus Atticae; et ubi Megaram*
   advēnit, eum occīdere cupīvit Scīrōn; is in <u>scopulō</u>
   <u>sedēbat</u>, et eōs <u>quī</u> trānsībant <u>pedēs</u> suōs <u>lavāre</u> iussit;
   et eōs, ubi id fēcērunt, <u>pedibus ā scopulō</u> in mare
5 *<u>dēiciēbat</u>. ibi habitābant <u>testūdinēs</u> ingentissimae; et*
   hae statim eōrum, quos <u>dēiciēbat</u> Scīrōn, corpora
   cōnsūmēbant; is Thēseum sīc occīdere cupīvit; sed
   Thēseus cum eō pugnāvit et eum <u>ipsum</u> in mare <u>dēiēcit</u>.
   tum Thēseus in Atticam advēnit; ibi <u>latrō</u>, Procrūstēs, sīc
10 *<u>hospitēs</u> occīdēbat: <u>lectum</u> habuit, in quō <u>hospes</u>*
   dormiēbat; eius, <u>quī</u> lectō longior erat, <u>membrōrum</u>
   partēs <u>abscīdēbat</u>; eius, <u>quī</u> lectō <u>brevior</u> erat, membra
   <u>distrahēbat</u>; sīc hospitēs suōs necābat; sīc tamen
   <u>latrōnem</u> Thēseus superāvit et occīdit.

scopulus, -ī, m. = rock, cliff
quī = who
sedeō, -ēre, sēdī, sessum = I sit
pēs, pedis, m. = foot
lavō, lavāre, lāvī, lautum =
   I wash
dēiciō, -ere, dēiēcī, dēiectum =
   I hurl down
testūdō, -inis, f. = tortoise
ipsum (acc. of ipse) = himself
latrō, -ōnis, m. = brigand
hospes, -itis, c. = guest, host
lectus, -ī, m. = bed
membrum, -ī, n. = limb
abscīdo, -ere, abscīdī,
   abscissum = I cut off
brevis, -e = short
distrahō, -ere, distrāxī,
   distractum = I pull asunder

Notes:

(i)   Attica (line 1) is a district in the south-east part of northern Greece; Athens was its capital.

(ii) Megara (line 1) is the city on the isthmus or narrow piece of land which joins Northern Greece to
      the Peloponnese (Southern Greece). It is sometimes feminine singular and sometimes neuter
      plural; take your choice!

(iii) *lătrō* (line 9) = 'a brigand';
      lātrō (with a long 'ā') = 'I bark'!

Exercise 10.11

Study the following passage (do not write a translation) and answer the questions below. Complete sentences are not required.

Theseus arrives in Athens

1 *Thēseus tandem <u>Athēnās</u> advēnit; ibi Aegeus, pater eius,*
   Mēdēam <u>dūxerat</u>; eī fīlium habuerant; hunc māter post
   patrem rēgem esse <u>Athēnārum</u> cupīvit; ea statim
   Thēseum <u>agnōvit</u> et coniugī suō dīxit: 'hic homō
5 *nostrōrum hostium amīcus est et nōs necāre cupit; sed*
   huic, antequam id faciet, vīnum <u>venēnātum</u> dabō.' et
   Thēseus <u>iam iam</u> vīnum bibēbat; sed pater eius gladium
   suum subitō cōnspexit, <u>quem</u> Thēseus tenēbat, et
   statim <u>pōculum</u> in <u>quō</u> vīnum erat ā <u>labrīs</u> eius <u>ēripuit</u> et
10 *ad terram <u>dēiēcit</u>. tum Thēseō, 'tū fīlius es meus,'*
   clāmāvit, 'et <u>hērēs</u> meus.' Mēdēam cum <u>fīliō</u> in <u>exilium</u>
   mīsit. posteā Thēseus saevissimum <u>taurum</u>, <u>quī</u>
   Marathōnem habitābat, occīdit. sīc in multīs locīs
   hominēs <u>mōnstrīs</u> crūdēlissimīs līberāvit et bonī omnēs
15 *eum magnopere laudāvērunt et amāvērunt.*

Athēnae, -ārum, f. pl = Athens
dūcō (here) = I marry
agnōscō, -ere, agnōvī, agnitum
   = I recognise
venēnātus, -a, -um = poisoned
iam iam bibēbat = was on the
   point of drinking
quem = which (acc.)
pōculum, -ī, n. = cup
quō = which (abl.)
labrum, -ī, n. = lip
ēripiō, -ere, ēripuī, ēreptum =
   I snatch away
dēiciō, -ere, dēiēcī, dēiectum =
   I hurl down
hērēs, hērēdis, c. = heir, heiress
exilium, -ī, n. = exile
taurus, -ī, m. = bull
quī = who
mōnstrum, -ī, n. (here) =
   monster

(a) In line 1, if *Athēnās* means 'to Athens', what sort of place must Athens be? This question requires two answers: 'either... or...'.

(b) In line 2, what is the tense of *dūxerat*?

(c) In line 5, what part of its verb is *necāre*? Is there any other example of this part in the passage?

(d) In line 8, can you think of any English word suggested by the verb *cōnspexit*? Explain the connexion between it and the Latin verb.

(e) Mention all the prepositions in this passage together with the words which they govern; and translate each example.

(f) In line 11, if, instead of 'he shouted', we wished to say 'he will shout', to what should we change *clāmāvit*?

(g) In line 14, if we wanted to say 'cruel' instead of 'very cruel', to what should we change *crūdēlissimīs*?

(h) In line 14, what English word do we 'understand' with *bonī*?

Notes:

(i) Soon after this Theseus went with the Athenian boys and girls, to face the Minotaur (see Book 1, Chapter 10, Exercise 10.10).

(ii) Medea was a terrifying lady, who started off as a sweet young girl, but was soon led into fearful ways by hard and treacherous men: she certainly gave as good as she got, though 'good' is hardly the right word.

(iii) Marathon is a famous old town in Attica. Hercules' seventh labour was to bring a fire-breathing bull from Crete to King Eurystheus in Mycenae (in the north of the Peloponnese). Eurystheus dedicated it to Juno, but she, because of her hatred of Hercules, chased it from place to place until it ended up, as a not very welcome guest, in Marathon.

N.B. *lăbrum, -ī*, n. = 'lip'; *lābrum, -ī*, n. = 'vat, tub'. And two more compound verbs for you: *ēripiō* is a compound of *rapiō* = 'I seize'; *dēicio* is a compound of *iaciō* = 'I throw' (see p. 56).

Exercise 10.12

Using the vocabulary given below, translate into Latin:

(i)   We are attacking the big town.

I attack = *oppugnō* (1); big = *magnus, -a, -um;* town = *oppidum, -ī,* n.

(ii)   The little girls were advising the good poet.

little = *parvus, -a, -um;* girl = *puella, -ae,* f; I advise = *moneō* (2); good = *bonus, -a, -um;* poet = *poēta, -ae,* m.

Exercise 10.13

1		2	3	4	5		6
		7					
8	9						
10			11		12	13	
14		15			16		17
18					19		
	20		21	22		23	
24			25		26		
		27					
28							

Across
 1. After (+ clause) (8)
 7. 'is or 'ers – dropping aitches, eh? (4)
 8. Add '-*mus*' and we shall stand (5)
10. 3 down's nominative (2)
11. You (sing.) are eating it when I sat backwards (2, 2)

14. A horse without an ending? (3)
16. Surely not? (3)
18. Or (3)
19. By the way (3)
20. Of my (fem. sing.), backwards (4)
23. Not out (2)
25. To the clever ones (*miaow*?)
27. With a nut reversed (4)
28. Before (+ clause) (8)

Down
 1. Afterwards (6)
 2. (With) one's own (fem. sing.) (3)
 3. To you (sing.) (4)
 4. What? (4)
 5. An ending for a horse (see 14 across) (2)
 6. After no long time (3)
 9. Caesar might have said this to Brutus (5)
12. Behold! Five (2, 1)
13. I sewed, I went (3, 2)
15. Three fifths of a sailor (3)
17. Remain supine (6)
21. Lo! or behold! (4)
22. 'Than' upside down (4)
24. My (girl) (3)
26. They rule backwards without their stem (3)
27. And there we are! (2)

The following vocabulary will help you:

aut = or
catus, -a, -um = clever
edō*, ēsse, ēdī, ēsum = I eat
ēn, ecce = lo! behold!
nux, nucis, f. = nut
sedeō, -ēre, sēdī, sessum = I sit
suō, -ere, suī, sūtum = I sew

* The 2ⁿᵈ person singular is *ēs*, not to be mixed up with *es* = 'you are' (sing.), from *sum* with a short '*e*'. Quantities are dogging us to the very end!

Vocabulary 10

Vocabulary 10

eō, -īre, iī/īvī, itum = I go

exeō, exīre, exiī, exitum = I go out

ineō, inīre, iniī, initum = I go in, enter

pereō, perīre, periī, peritum = I perish

trānseō, trānsīre, trānsiī, trānsitum = I cross

possum, posse, potuī = I am able

pūniō, -īre, -īvī, -ītum = I punish

virtūs, virtūtis, f. = virtue, esp. courage

parēns, -entis, c. = parent

redeō, redīre, rediī, reditum = I return (intr.)

nōnne? expects answer 'yes'

num? expects answer 'no'

nēmō (irregular) = nobody

nihil = nothing

You have probably noticed that we have been eking this chapter out for as long a time as we can. But alas! this really is it. However, look now to the glorious future and order your copies of Book 3 in good time to avoid disappointment.

Meanwhile,

valēte!

Proper nouns and adjectives

Achillēs, Achillis, m. = Achilles (a Greek hero)

Actium, -ī, n. = Actium (a town in Greece, famous for the Battle of Actium in 31 B.C.)

Aegeus, -ī, m. = Aegeus (a king of Athens, father of Theseus)

Aegyptus, -ī, f. = Egypt

Aethra, -ae, f. = Aethra (mother of Theseus)

Agamemnōn, -onis, m. = Agamemnon (chief king of the Greeks)

Agrippa, -ae, m. = Agrippa (a friend of Octavian's)

Agrippīna, -ae, f. = Agrippina (wife of the emperor Claudius)

Antōnius, Antōniī, m. = Antony (rival of Octavian)

Apollō, Apollinis, m. = Apollo (the god of prophecy)

Athēnae, -ārum, f. pl. = Athens (a city in Greece)

Atia, -ae, f. = Atia (mother of Octavian)

Attica, -ae, f. = Attica (a district in Greece)

Augustus, -ī, m. = Augustus (name assumed by Octavian)

Aulis, Aulidis, f. = Aulis (a port in Greece)

Bacchus, -ī, m. = Bacchus (the god of wine)

Bellerophōn, -ontis, m. = Bellerophon (a Greek hero)

Britannia, -ae, f. = Britain

Brūtus, -ī, m. = Brutus (one-time friend, later assassin of Julius Caesar)

Caesar, Caesaris, m. = Caesar (a famous Roman statesman)

Caligula, -ae, m. = Caligula (a Roman emperor)

Calliopēa, -ae, f. = Calliopea (one of the Muses)

Capreae, -ārum, f. pl. = Capri (an island off the coast of Italy)

Cassius, -ī, m. = Cassius

Cerberus, -ī, m. = Cerberus (a three-headed dog that guarded the Underworld)

Chaerea, -ae, m. = Chaerea (assassin of the emperor Caligula)

Charōn, -ōnis, m. = Charon (the ferryman of the Underworld)

Chimaera, -ae, f. = the Chimacra (a monster)

Claudius, -ī, m. = Claudius (a Roman emperor)

Cleopatra, -ae, f. = Cleopatra (a queen of Egypt)

Clytaemnēstra, -ae, f. = Clytemnestra (wife of Agamemnon)

Corinthus, -ī, f. = Corinth (a city in Greece)

Croesus, -ī, m. = Croesus (a king of Lydia, famed for his riches)

Cȳrus, -ī, m. = Cyrus (a king of Persia)

Delphī, -ōrum, m. pl. = Delphi (site of the oracle of Apollo in central Greece)

Diāna, -ae, f. = Diana (goddess of hunting)

Eurydicē, -ēs (Greek declension*), f. = Eurydice (wife of Orpheus)

Gallia, -ae, f. = Gaul (roughly modern-day France)

Hebrus, -ī, m. = Hebrus (a river in Thrace)

Helena, -ae, f. = Helen (wife of Menelaus)

Ībycus, -ī, m. = Ibycus (a Greek poet)

Incitātus, -ī, m. = Incitatus (a horse of the emperor Caligula's)

Īobatēs, -is, m. = Iobates (a king of Lycia)

Īphigenīa, -ae, f. = Iphigenia (daughter of Agamemnon and Clytemnestra)

Iūlia, -ae, f. = Julia (grandmother of Octavian)

Iūlius, Iūliī, m. = Julius

Iuppiter, Iovis, m. = Jupiter (king of the gods)

Lesbus, -ī, f. = Lesbos (an island in the Aegean sea)

Lycia, -ae, f. = Lycia (a country in Asia Minor)

Lȳdia, -ae, f. = Lydia (a country in Asia Minor)

Marathōn, -ōnis, f. = Marathon (a town in Greece)

Mēdēa, -ae, f. = Medea (wife of Aegeus)

Megara, -ae, f. = Megara (a city in Greece)

Menelāus, -ī, m. = Menelaus (a king of Sparta)

Minerva, -ae, f. = Minerva (the goddess of wisdom)

Mūsa, -ae, f. = a Muse (one of the nine goddesses who were patrons of the arts)

Mycēnae, -ārum, f. pl. = Mycenae (a city in Greece)

Narcissus, -ī, m. = Narcissus (a very handsome youth, now the name of a flower)

Neptūnus, -ī, m. = Neptune (the god of the sea)

Nerō, -ōnis, m. = Nero (a Roman emperor)

Octāviānus, -ī, m. = Octavian (later the emperor Augustus)

Octāvius, Octāviī, m. = Octavius (father of Octavian)

Olympus, *-ī*, m. = Olympus (a mountain in Greece, home of the gods)

Orpheus, *-ī*, m. = Orpheus (a famous Greek musician)

Paris, *Paridis*, m. = Paris (son of the king of Troy)

Pēgasus, *-ī*, m. = Pegasus (a winged horse)

Persae, *-ārum*, m. pl. = the Persians

Philippus, *-ī*, m. = Philippus (Octavian's step-father)

Philonoē, *-ēs* (Greek declension*), f. = Philonoe (daughter of Iobates)

Plūtō, *-ōnis*, m. = Pluto (the god of the Underworld)

Priamus, *-ī*, m. = Priam (a king of Troy)

Procrūstēs, *-ae* (Greek declension*), m. = Procrustes (a cruel brigand)

Proetus, *-ī*, m. = Proetus (a king of Tiryns)

Prōserpina, *-ae*, f. = Proserpina (wife of Pluto)

Rōma, *-ae*, f. = Rome

Scīrōn, *Scīrōnis*, m. = Sciron (a cruel brigand)

Sinis, *Sinis*, m. = Sinis (a cruel robber)

Solō, *Solōnis*, m. = Solon (an Athenian lawgiver and philosopher)

Sparta, *-ae*, f. = Sparta (a city in Greece)

Suētōnius, *-ī*, m. = Suetonius (a Roman biographer)

Tacitus, *-ī*, m. = Tacitus (a Roman historian)

Tartarus, *-ī*, m. = Tartarus (the Underworld)

Thēseus, *Thēseī*, m. = Theseus (a Greek hero)

Thrācia, *-ae*, f. = Thrace (a large region to the north of Greece)

Tiberius, *-ī*, m. = Tiberius (a Roman emperor)

Tirȳns, *Tirynthis*, f. = Tiryns (a city in Greece)

Troezēn, *Troezēnis*, f. = Troezen (a city in Greece)

Troia, *-ae*, f. = Troy (a city in Asia Minor)

Troiānus, *-a*, *-um* = Trojan

* Some nouns of Greek origin, especially proper nouns, exist in their Greek forms. Pupils are not required to learn the declension of such nouns.

Names should always be translated into their nominative forms.

e.g.   *Thēseī* = 'of Theseus'
       nēmō Tiberium amat = 'no one loves Tiberius'

Some nouns are so familiar that we Anglicise them.

e.g.   *Corinthus* = Corinth
       Helena = Helen
       Priamus = Priam

Vocabulary: Latin-English

ā, ab (+ abl.) = by, from
absum, abesse, āfuī (goes like *sum*) = I am absent
accipiō, -ere, accēpī, acceptum = I receive
ad (+ acc.) = to, towards
adsum, adesse, adfuī (goes like *sum*) = I am present
adveniō, -īre, advēnī, adventum = I arrive, come to
aedificō, -āre, -āvī, -ātum = I build
ager, agrī, m. = field
agricola, -ae, m. = farmer
altus, -a, -um = high, deep
ambulō, -āre, -āvī, -ātum = I walk
amīcus, -ī, m. = friend
amō, amāre, amāvī, amātum = I love, like
ancilla, -ae, f. = maid-servant
ante (+ acc.) = before (preposition)
antequam = before (conjunction)
appropinquō, -āre, -āvī, -ātum (+ dat. or *ad* + acc.) = I approach
aqua, -ae, f. = water
arma, -ōrum, n. pl. = weapons
audāx, audācis = bold
audiō, -īre, -īvī, -ītum = I hear, listen to
aurum, -ī, n. = gold
autem = however, moreover (not written 1st word in sentence)
auxilium, -iī, n. = help
bellum, -ī, n. = war
bene = well
bibō, -ere, bibī = I drink
bonus, -a, -um = good
caelum, -ī, n. = sky
cantō, -āre, -āvī, -ātum = I sing
capiō, -ere, cēpī, captum = I take, capture
cārus, -a, -um = dear
celeriter = quickly
cēterī, -ae, -a = other, remaining
cibus, -ī, m. = food
circum (+ acc.) = around
cīvis, cīvis, c. = citizen
clāmō, -āre, -āvī, -ātum = I shout
clāmor, -ōris, m. = shout

clārus, -a, -um = famous, clear, bright
colligō, -ere, collēgī, collēctum = I collect
comes, comitis, c. = companion
coniūnx, coniugis, c. = husband/wife
cōnspiciō, -ere, cōnspexī, cōnspectum = I catch sight of
cōnstituō, -ere, cōnstituī, cōnstitūtum = I decide, settle
cōnsūmō, -ere, cōnsūmpsī, cōnsūmptum = I eat, consume
contrā (+ acc.) = against
cōpiae, -ārum, f. pl. = forces
corpus, -oris, n. = body
crās = tomorrow
crūdēlis, -e = cruel
cum (+ abl.) = with, together with
cupiō, -ere, -īvī, -ītum = I want, desire
cūr? = why?
currō, -ere, cucurrī, cursum = I run
dē (+ abl.) = down from, concerning
dea, -ae, f. = goddess (dat. and abl. pl. = *deābus*)
decem = ten
decimus, -a, -um = tenth
dēfendō, -ere, dēfendī, dēfēnsum = I defend
deinde = then, next
dēleō, dēlēre, dēlēvī, dēlētum = I destroy
deus, deī, m. (irreg.) = god
dīcō, dīcere, dīxī, dictum = I say
difficilis, -e = difficult
discēdō, -ere, discessī, discessum = I depart
diū (adverb) = for a long time
dō, dāre, dedī, dătum = I give
dominus, -ī, m. = master, lord
dōnum, -ī, n. = gift
dormiō, -īre, -īvī, -ītum = I sleep
dūcō, -ere, dūxī, ductum = I lead
duo, duae, duo = two
duodecim = twelve
duodēvīgintī = eighteen
dux, ducis, c. = leader
ē, ex (+ abl.) = out of
effugiō, -ere, effugī = I escape
ego = I
eō, īre, iī (or *īvī*), *itum* (irreg.) = I go

equus, equī, m. = horse
errō, -āre, -āvī, -ātum = I wander
et = and
et...et = both...and
etiam = even, also
ex (+ abl.) = out of
exeō, exīre, exiī, exitum (goes like *eō*) = I go out
exspectō, -āre, -āvī, -ātum = I wait for
facilis, -e = easy
faciō, -ere, fēcī, factum = I do, make
fēlīx, fēlīcis = fortunate, happy, lucky
fēmina, -ae, f. = woman
fessus, -a, -um = tired
festīnō, -āre, -āvī, -ātum = I hurry
filia, -ae, f. = daughter (dat. and abl. pl. = *filiābus*)
filius, filiī (or *filī*), m. (irreg.) = son
flūmen, flūminis, n. = river
forte = by chance
fortis, -e = brave, strong
fortiter = bravely
frāter, frātris, m. = brother
frūstrā = in vain
fugiō, -ere, fūgī, fugitum = I flee, flee from
gerō, -ere, gessī, gestum = I carry on, do, wear
    (+ *bellum* = I wage a war)
gladius, gladiī, m. = sword
Graecus, -a, -um = Greek
habeō, -ēre, -uī, -itum = I have
habitō, -āre, -āvī, -ātum = I live, inhabit
hasta, -ae, f. = spear
herī = yesterday
hīc = here
hic, haec, hoc = this; he, she, it
hodiē = today
homō, hominis, c. = person, man
hostis, hostis, c. = enemy (usually used in plural)
iaciō, -ere, iēcī, iactum = I throw
iam = now, already
ibi = there
igitur = therefore (not generally written 1st word in sentence)
ille, illa, illud = that; he, she, it
in (+ abl.) = in, on
in (+ acc.) = into, on to
incola, -ae, c. = inhabitant
ineō, inīre, iniī, initum (goes like *eō*) = I go in, enter
ingēns, ingentis = huge
īnsula, -ae, f. = island
inter (+ acc.) = between, among

intrō, -āre, -āvī, -ātum = I enter
inveniō, -īre, invēnī, inventum = I find
īra, -ae, f. = anger
īrātus, -a, -um = angry
is, ea, id = that; he, she, it
itaque = therefore
iter, itineris, n. = journey
iterum = again
iubeō, -ēre, iussī, iussum = I order
iuvenis, iuvenis, c. = young person, young man
labōrō, -āre, -āvī, -ātum = I work
laetus, -a, -um = happy
laudō, -āre, -āvī, -ātum = I praise
legō, -ere, lēgī, lēctum = I read, choose
liber, librī, m. = book
līberō, -āre, -āvī, -ātum = I free
locus, -ī, m. = place
longus, -a, -um = long
lūdō, -ere, lūsī, lūsum = I play
lūx, lūcis, f. = light
magister, magistrī, m. = master, schoolmaster, teacher
magnopere = greatly
magnus, -a, -um = big, great
malus, -a, -um = bad
maneō, -ēre, mānsī, mānsum = I remain
mare, maris, n. = sea
māter, mātris, f. = mother
medius, -a, -um = middle (of)
melior, melius = better
meus, -a, -um = my
mīles, mīlitis, c. = soldier
miser, -era, -erum = wretched
mittō, -ere, mīsī, missum = I send
moneō, -ēre, -uī, -itum = I warn, advise
mōns, montis, m. = mountain
mora, -ae, f. = delay
mors, mortis, f. = death
mortuus, -a, -um = dead
moveō, -ēre, mōvī, mōtum = I move (trans.)
mox = soon
mulier, mulieris, f. = woman
multus, -a, -um = much, many
mūrus, -ī, m. = wall
nam = for
nārrō, -āre, -āvī, -ātum = I tell
nauta, -ae, m. = sailor
nāvigō, -āre, -āvī, -ātum = I sail
nāvis, nāvis, f. (abl. sing. = *nāvī* or *nāve*)
    = ship

-ne?: introduces a question

necō, necāre, necāvī, necātum = I kill

nēmō (acc. = *nēminem*; dat. = *nēminī*), c. = no one

nihil = nothing

nōbilis, -e = noble, famous

nōlī / nōlīte (+ infin.) = do not!

nōmen, nōminis, n. = name

nōn = not

nōnne?: introduces a question (expecting the answer 'yes')

nōnus -a, -um = ninth

nōs = we

noster, nostra, nostrum = our

nōtus, -a, -um = well-known

novem = nine

novus, -a, -um = new

num?: introduces a question (expecting the answer 'no')

numquam = never

nunc = now

nūntiō, -āre, -āvī, -ātum = I report, announce

nūntius, nūntiī, m. = messenger, message

occīdō, -ere, occīdī, occīsum = I kill

occupō, -āre, -āvī, -ātum = I seize (a place)

octāvus, -a, -um = eighth

octō = eight

ōlim = once upon a time

omnis, -e = every, all, the whole (of)

oppidum, -ī, n. = town

oppugnō, -āre, -āvī, -ātum = I attack (a place)

optimus, -a, -um = best

ostendō, -ere, ostendī, ostēnsum / ostentum = I show

parēns, parentis, c. = parent

parō, -āre, -āvī, -ātum = I prepare

pars, partis, f. = part

parvus, -a, -um = small, little

pater, patris, m. = father

patria, -ae, f. = country, fatherland

paucī, -ae, -a = few

pecūnia, -ae, f. = money

peior, peius = worse

per (+ acc.) = through, along

pereō, -īre, periī, peritum (goes like *eō*) = I die

perīculum, -ī, n. = danger

perterritus, -a, -um = terrified, frightened

pessimus, -a, -um = worst

poēta, -ae, m. = poet

pōnō, -ere, posuī, positum = I place

portō, -āre, -āvī, -ātum = I carry

possum, posse, potuī (irreg.) = I am able

post (+ acc.) = after (preposition)

posteā = afterwards

postquam = after (conjunction)

prīmus, -a, -um = first

prō (+ abl.) = on behalf of, in place of, in front of, instead of

proelium, -iī, n. = battle

prope (+ acc.) = near

propter (+ acc.) = on account of, because of

puella, -ae, f. = girl

puer, puerī, m. = boy

pugnō, -āre, -āvī, -ātum = I fight

pulcher, pulchra, pulchrum = beautiful

pūniō, -īre, -īvī, -ītum = I punish

quam = than

quamquam = although

quārtus, -a, -um = fourth

quattuor = four

quattuordecim = fourteen

-que = and

quid? = what?

quīndecim = fifteen

quīnque = five

quīntus, -a, -um = fifth

quis? = who?

quod = because

quoque = also (comes after the word it is emphasising)

redeō, redīre, rediī, reditum (goes like *eō*) = I go back, return

redūcō, -ere, redūxī, reductum = I lead back

rēgīna, -ae, f. = queen

regō, -ere, rēxī, rēctum = I rule

respondeō, -ēre, respondī, respōnsum = I reply, answer

rēx, rēgis, m. = king

rīdeō, -ere, rīsī, rīsum = I laugh, laugh at, smile

rogō, -āre, -āvī, -ātum = I ask, ask for

Rōmānus, -a, -um = Roman (adjective)

ruō, ruere, ruī, rutum = I rush, collapse, charge

sacer, sacra, sacrum = sacred

saepe = often

saevus, -a, -um = savage, fierce

sagitta, -ae, f. = arrow

salūtō, -āre, -āvī, -ātum = I greet

sapiēns, sapientis = wise

scrībō, -ere, scrīpsī, scrīptum = I write

scūtum, -ī, n. = shield

sē = himself, herself, itself, themselves (reflexive pronoun)

secundus, -a, -um = second

sed = but

sēdecim = sixteen

semper = always

senex, senis, m. = old man

septem = seven

septendecim = seventeen

septimus, -a, -um = seventh

servō, -āre, -āvī, -ātum = I save

servus, -ī, m. = slave

sex = six

sextus, -a, -um = sixth

sīc = thus

sine (+ abl.) = without

socius, -ī, m. = ally

sōlus, -a, -um (like *ūnus*) = alone

soror, -ōris, f. = sister

spectō, -āre, -āvī, -ātum = I watch

statim = immediately

stō, stāre, stetī, stătum = I stand

sub (+ abl.) = under

subitō = suddenly

sum, esse, fuī (irreg.) = I am

super (+ acc.) = over

superō, -āre, -āvī, -ātum = I overcome

suus, sua, suum = his (own), her (own), its (own), their (own)

tamen = however (not generally written first word in sentence)

tandem = at last

templum, -ī, n. = temple

teneō, -ēre, tenuī, tentum = I hold

terra, -ae, f. = land, earth

terreō, -ēre, -uī, -ītum = I terrify, frighten

tertius, -a, -um = third

timeō, -ēre, -uī = I fear

trādō, -ere, trādidī, trāditum = I hand over

trāns (+ acc.) = across

trānseō, -īre, -iī, -itum (goes like *eō*) = I go across

tredecim = thirteen

trēs, tria = three

trīstis, trīste = sad, gloomy

tū = you (singular)

tum = then

turba, -ae, f. = crowd

tūtus, -a, -um = safe

tuus, -a, -um = your (belonging to you [sing.])

ubi = when

ubi? = where?

unda, -ae, f. = wave

ūndecim = eleven

ūndēvīgintī = nineteen

ūnus, -a, -um (gen. sing. = *ūnīus*, dat. sing. = *ūnī*) = one, only one

urbs, urbis, f. = city

uxor, -ōris, f. = wife

validus, -a, -um = strong

veniō, -īre, vēnī, ventum = I come

ventus, -ī, m. = wind

verbum, -ī, n. = word

vester, vestra, vestrum = your (belonging to you [pl.])

via, -ae, f. = road, street, way

videō, -ēre, vīdī, vīsum = I see

vīgintī = twenty

vincō, -ere, vīcī, victum = I conquer

vīnum, -ī, n. = wine

vir, virī, m. (irreg.) = man (as opposed to woman)

virtūs, virtūtis, f. = courage

vīvus, -a, -um = alive

vocō, -āre, -āvī, -ātum = I call

vōs = you (plural)

vōx, vōcis, f. = voice

vulnerō, -āre, -āvī, -ātum = I wound

vulnus, vulneris, n. = wound

Vocabulary: English-Latin

Able, I am = *possum, posse, potuī* (irreg.)

About = *dē* (+ abl.)

Absent, I am = *absum, abesse, āfuī* (goes like *sum*)

Across = *trāns* (+ acc.)

Advise, I = *moneō, -ēre, -uī, -itum*

Afraid, I am = *timeō, -ēre, -uī*

Afraid = *perterritus, -a, -um*

After (conjunction) = *postquam*

After (preposition) = *post* (+ acc.)

Afterwards = *posteā*

Again = *iterum*

Against = *contrā* (+ acc.)

Alive = *vīvus, -a, -um*

All, every = *omnis, -e*

Ally = *socius, -iī*, m.

Alone = *sōlus, -a, -um* (like *ūnus*)

Along = *per* (+ acc.)

Already = *iam*

Also = *etiam*; *quoque* (comes after the word it is emphasising)

Although = *quamquam*

Always = *semper*

Am, I = *sum, esse, fuī* (irreg.)

Among = *inter* (+ acc.)

And = *et*; *-que*

Anger = *īra, -ae*, f.

Angry = *īrātus, -a, -um*

Approach, I = *appropinquō, -āre, -āvī, -ātum* (+ dat. or *ad* + acc.)

Around = *circum* (+ acc.)

Arrive, I = *adveniō, -īre, advēnī, adventum*

Arrow = *sagitta, -ae*, f.

Ask, I = *rogō, -āre, -āvī, -ātum*

At last = *tandem*

Attack (a place), I = *oppugnō, -āre, -āvī, -ātum*

Bad = *malus, -a, -um*

Battle = *proelium, -iī*, n.

Beautiful = *pulcher, pulchra, pulchrum*

Because = *quod*

Because of = *propter* (+ acc.)

Before (conjunction) = *antequam*

Before (preposition) = *ante* (+ acc.)

Best = *optimus, -a, -um*

Better = *melior, melius*

Between = *inter* (+ acc.)

Big = *magnus, -a, -um*

Body = *corpus, -oris*, n.

Bold = *audāx, audācis*

Book = *liber, librī*, m.

Both…and = *et…et*

Boy = *puer, puerī*, m.

Brave = *fortis, -e*

Bravely = *fortiter*

Brother = *frāter, frātris*, m.

Build, I = *aedificō, -āre, -āvī, -ātum*

But = *sed*

By chance = *forte*

By, from = *ā, ab* (+ abl.)

Call, I = *vocō, -āre, -āvī, -ātum*

Capture I = *capiō, -ere, cēpī, captum*

Carry, I = *portō, -āre, -āvī, -ātum*

Catch sight of, I = *cōnspiciō, -ere, cōnspexī, cōnspectum*

Choose, I = *legō, -ere, lēgī, lēctum*

Citizen = *cīvis, cīvis*, c.

City = *urbs, urbis*, f.

Clear = *clārus, -a, -um*

Collect, I = *colligō, -ere, collēgī, collēctum*

Come, I = *veniō, -īre, vēnī, ventum*

Companion = *comes, comitis*, c.

Conquer, I = *vincō, -ere, vīcī, victum*

Country = *patria, -ae*, f.

Courage = *virtūs, virtūtis*, f.

Crowd = *turba, -ae*, f.

Cruel = *crūdēlis, -e*

Danger = *perīculum, -ī*, n.

Daughter = *fīlia, -ae*, f. (dat. and abl. pl. = *fīliābus*)

Dead = *mortuus, -a, -um*

Dear = *cārus, -a, -um*

Death = *mors, mortis*, f.

Decide, I = *cōnstituō, -ere, cōnstituī, cōnstitūtum*

Deep = *altus, -a, -um*

Defend, I = *dēfendō, -ere, dēfendī, dēfēnsum*

Delay = *mōra, -ae*, f.

Depart, I = *discēdō, -ere, discessī, discessum*

Desire, I = *cupiō, -ere, -īvī, -ītum*

Destroy, I = *dēleō, dēlēre, dēlēvī, dēlētum*

Die, I = *pereō, -īre, periī, peritum* (goes like *eō*)

Difficult = *difficilis, -e*

Do not…! = *nōlī / nōlīte* (+ infin.)

Do, I = *faciō, -ere, fēcī, factum*

Down from = *dē* (+ abl.)

Drink, I = *bibō, -ere, bibī*

Earth = *terra, -ae*, f.

Easy = *facilis, -e*

Eat, I = *cōnsūmō, -ere, cōnsūmpsī, cōnsūmptum*

Eight = *octō*

Eighteen = *duodēvīgintī*

Eighth = *octāvus, -a, -um*

Eleven = *ūndecim*

Enemy = *hostis, hostis*, c. (usually used in plural)

Enter, I = *intrō, -āre, -āvī, -ātum*

Escape, I = *effugiō, -ere, effūgī*

Even = *etiam*

Every = *omnis, -e*

Famous = *clārus, -a, -um; nōtus, -a, -um*

Farmer = *agricola, -ae*, m.

Father = *pater, patris*, m.

Fatherland = *patria, -ae*, f.

Fear, I = *timeō, -ere, -uī*

Few = *paucī, -ae, -a*

Field = *ager, agrī*, m.

Fifteen = *quīndecim*

Fifth = *quīntus, -a, -um*

Fight, I = *pugnō, -āre, -āvī, -ātum*

Find, I = *inveniō, -īre, invēnī, inventum*

First = *prīmus, -a, -um*

Five = *quīnque*

Flee (from), I = *fugiō, -ere, fūgī, fugitum*

Food = *cibus, -ī*, m.

For = *nam*

For a long time = *diū* (adverb)

Forces = *cōpiae, -ārum*, f. pl.

Fortunate = *fēlīx, fēlīcis*

Four = *quattuor*

Fourteen = *quattuordecim*

Fourth = *quārtus, -a, -um*

Free, I = *līberō, -āre, -āvī, -ātum*

Friend = *amīcus, -ī*, m.

Frightened = *perterritus, -a, -um*

From = *ā, ab* (+ abl.)

General = *dux, ducis*, c.

Gift = *dōnum, -ī*, n.

Girl = *puella, -ae*, f.

Gloomy = *trīstīs, -e*

Give, I = *dō, dăre, dedī, dătum*

Go, I = *eō, īre, iī* (or *īvī*), *itum* (irreg.)

Go across, I = *trānseō, -īre, -iī, -itum* (goes like *eō*)

Go back, I = *redeō, redīre, rediī, reditum* (goes like *eō*)

Go in, I = *ineō, inīre, iniī, initum* (goes like *eō*)

Go out, I = *exeō, exīre, exiī, exitum* (goes like *eō*)

God = *deus, deī*, m. (irreg.)

Goddess = *dea, -ae*, f. (dat. and abl. pl. = *deābus*)

Gold = *aurum, -ī*, n.

Good = *bonus, -a, -um*

Great = *magnus, -a, -um*

Greatly = *magnopere*

Greek = *Graecus, -a, -um*

Greet, I = *salūtō, -āre, -āvī, -ātum*

Hand over, I = *trādō, -ere, trādidī, trāditum*

Happy = *laetus, -a, -um*

Have, I = *habeō, -ēre, -uī, -itum*

Hear, I = *audiō, -īre, -īvī, -ītum*

Help = *auxilium, -iī*, n.

Her (own) = *suus, sua, suum*

Here = *hīc*

Herself (reflexive) = *sē*

High = *altus, -a, -um*

Himself (reflexive) = *sē*

His (own) = *suus, sua, suum*

Hold, I = *teneō, -ēre, tenuī, tentum*

Horse = *equus, equī*, m.

However = *tamen* (not generally written first word in sentence)

Huge = *ingēns, ingentis*

Hurry, I = *festīnō, -āre, -āvī, -ātum*

Husband = *coniūnx, coniugis*, m.

I = *ego*

Immediately = *statim*

In = *in* (+ abl.)

In front of = *prō* (+ abl.)

In vain = *frūstrā*

Inhabit, I = *habitō, -āre, -āvī, -ātum*

Inhabitant = *incola, -ae*, c.

Into = *in* (+ acc.)

Island = *īnsula, -ae*, f.

Itself (reflexive) = *sē*

Journey = *iter, itineris*, n.

Kill, I = *necō, necāre, necāvī, necātum; occīdō, -ere, occīdī, occīsum*

King = *rēx, rēgis*, m.

Land = *terra, -ae*, f.

Laugh, I = *rīdeō, -ēre, rīsī, rīsum*

Lead, I = *dūcō, -ere, dūxī, ductum*

Lead back, I = *redūcō, -ere, redūxī, reductum*

Leader = *dux, ducis*, c.

Light = *lūx, lūcis*, f.
Like, I = *amō, amāre, amāvī, amātum*
Listen to, I = *audiō, -īre,-īvī, -ītum*
Live (inhabit), I = *habitō, -āre, -āvī, -ātum*
Long = *longus, -a, -um*
Look at, I = *spectō, -āre, -āvī, -ātum*
Lord = *dominus, -ī*, m.
Love, I = *amō, amāre, amāvī, amātum*
Lucky = *fēlīx, fēlīcis*
Maid-servant = *ancilla, -ae*, f.
Make, I = *faciō, -ere, fēcī, factum*
Man (as opposed to woman) = *vir, virī*, m. (irreg.)
Man (person) = *homō, hominis*, c.
Many: see 'much'
Master, lord = *dominus, -ī*, m.
Master, teacher = *magister, magistrī*, m.
Message = *nūntius, nūntiī*, m.
Messenger = *nūntius, nūntiī*, m.
Middle (of) = *medius, -a, -um*
Miserable = *miser, -era, -erum*
Money = *pecūnia, -ae*, f.
Moreover = *autem* (not written 1st word in sentence)
Mother = *māter, mātris*, f.
Mountain = *mōns, montis*, m.
Move (trans.), I = *moveō, -ēre, mōvī, mōtum*
Much = *multus, -a, -um*
My = *meus, -a, -um*
Name = *nōmen, nōminis*, n.
Near = *prope* (+ acc.)
Never = *numquam*
New = *novus, -a, -um*
Nine = *novem*
Nineteen = *ūndēvīgintī*
Ninth = *nōnus, -a, -um*
No one = *nēmō* (acc. = *nēminem*; dat. = *nēminī*), c.
Noble = *nōbilis, -e*
Not = *nōn*
Nothing = *nihil*
Now = *nunc; iam*
Often = *saepe*
Old man = *senex, senis*, m.
On = *in* (+ abl.)
On account of = *propter* (+ acc.)
On behalf of = *prō* (+ abl.)
On to = *in* (+ acc.)
Once upon a time = *ōlim*
One = *ūnus, -a, -um* (gen. sing. = *ūnīus*, dat. sing. = *ūnī*)
Order, I = *iubeō, -ēre, iussī, iussum*
Other, remaining = *cēterī, -ae, -a*

Our = *noster, nostra, nostrum*
Out of = *ex, ē* (+ abl.)
Over = *super* (+ acc.)
Overcome, I = *superō, -āre, -āvī, -ātum*
Parent = *parēns, parentis*, c.
Part = *pars, partis*, f.
Place, a = *locus, -ī*, m.
Place, I = *pōnō, -ere, posuī, positum*
Play, I = *lūdō, -ere, lūsī, lūsum*
Poet = *poēta, -ae*, m.
Praise, I = *laudō, -āre, -āvī, -ātum*
Prepare, I = *parō, -āre, -āvī, -ātum*
Present, I am = *adsum, adesse, adfuī* (goes like *sum*)
Punish, I = *pūniō, -īre, -īvī, -ītum*
Queen = *rēgīna, -ae*, f.
Quickly = *celeriter*
Read, I = *legō, -ere, lēgī, lēctum*
Receive, I = *accipiō, -ere, accēpī, acceptum*
Remain, I = *maneō, -ēre, mānsī, mānsum*
Reply, I = *respondeō, -ēre, respondī, respōnsum*
Report, I = *nūntiō, -āre, -āvī, -ātum*
Rest of = *cēterī, -ae, -a*
River = *flūmen, flūminis*, n.
Road = *via, -ae*, f.
Roman = *Rōmānus, -a, -um*
Rule, I = *regō, -ere, rēxī, rēctum*
Run, I = *currō, -ere, cucurrī, cursum*
Rush, I = *ruō, ruere, ruī, rutum*
Sacred = *sacer, sacra, sacrum*
Sad = *trīstis, trīste*
Safe = *tūtus, -a, -um*
Sail, I = *nāvigō, -āre, -āvī, -ātum*
Sailor = *nauta, -ae*, m.
Savage = *saevus, -a, -um*
Save, I = *servō, -āre, -āvī, -ātum*
Say, I = *dīcō, dīcere, dīxī, dictum*
Sea = *mare, maris*, n.
Second = *secundus, -a, -um*
See, I = *videō, -ēre, vīdī, vīsum*
Seize (a place), I = *occupō, -āre, -āvī, -ātum*
Send, I = *mittō, -ere, mīsī, missum*
Seven = *septem*
Seventeen = *septendecim*
Seventh = *septimus, -a, -um*
Shield = *scūtum, -ī*, n.
Ship = *nāvis, nāvis*, f. (abl. sing. = *nāvī* or *nāve*)
Shout, a = *clāmor, -ōris*, m.
Shout, I = *clāmō, -āre, -āvī, -ātum*
Show, I = *ostendō, -ere, ostendī, ostēnsum/ostentum*

Sing, I = *cantō, -āre, -āvī, -ātum*
Sister = *soror, -ōris,* f.
Six = *sex*
Sixteen = *sēdecim*
Sixth = *sextus, -a, -um*
Sky = *caelum, -ī,* n.
Slave = *servus, -ī,* m.
Sleep, I = *dormiō, -īre, -īvī, -ītum*
Small = *parvus, -a, -um*
Smile, I = *rīdeō, -ēre, rīsī, rīsum*
Soldier = *mīles, mīlitis,* c.
Son = *fīlius, fīliī* (or *fīlī*), m. (irreg.)
Soon = *mox*
Spear = *hasta, -ae,* f.
Stand, I = *stō, stāre, stetī, stătum*
Street = *via, -ae,* f.
Strong = *validus, -a, -um*
Suddenly = *subitō*
Surely… = *nōnne?* (introduces a question expecting
    the answer 'yes')
Surely…not = *num?* (introduces a question
    expecting the answer 'no')
Sword = *gladius, gladiī,* m.
Take, capture I = *capiō, -ere, cēpī, captum*
Teacher = *magister, magistrī,* m.
Tell, I = *nārrō, -āre, -āvī, -ātum*
Temple = *templum, -ī,* n.
Ten = *decem*
Tenth = *decimus*
Terrified = *perterritus, -a, -um*
Terrify, I = *terreō, -ēre, -uī, -itum*
Than = *quam*
That = *ille, illa, illud; is, ea, id*
Their (own) = *suus, sua, suum*
Themselves (reflexive) = *sē*
Then = *tum; deinde* (= next)
There = *ibi*
Therefore = *itaque; igitur* (not generally written 1st
    word in clause)
Third = *tertius, -a, -um*
Thirteen = *tredecim*
This = *hic, haec, hoc*
Three = *trēs, tria*
Through = *per* (+ acc.)
Throw, I = *iaciō, -ere, iēcī, iactum*
Thus = *sīc*
Tired = *fessus, -a, -um*
To, towards = *ad* (+ acc.)
Today = *hodiē*
Tomorrow = *crās*
Towards = *ad* (+ acc.)
Town = *oppidum, -ī,* n.

Twelve = *duodecim*
Twenty = *vīgintī*
Two = *duo, duae, duo*
Under = *sub* (+ abl.)
Voice = *vōx, vōcis,* f.
Wage (a war), I = *bellum gerō, -ere, gessī, gestum*
Wait for, I = *exspectō, -āre, -āvī, -ātum*
Walk, I = *ambulō, -āre, -āvī, -ātum*
Wall = *mūrus, -ī,* m.
Wander, I = *errō, -āre, -āvī, -ātum*
Want, I = *cupiō, -ere, -īvī, -ītum*
War = *bellum, -ī,* n.
Warn, I = *moneō, -ēre, -uī, -itum*
Watch, I = *spectō, -āre, -āvī, -ātum*
Water = *aqua, -ae,* f.
Wave = *unda, -ae,* f.
Way = *via, -ae,* f.
We = *nōs*
Weapons = *arma, -ōrum,* n. pl.
Well = *bene*
Well-known = *nōtus, -a, -um*
What? = *quid?*
When = *ubi*
Where? = *ubi?*
Who? = *quis?*
Whole (of) = *omnis, -e*
Why? = *cūr?*
Wicked = *malus, -a, -um*
Wife = *uxor, -ōris,* f.; *coniūnx, coniugis,* f.
Wind = *ventus, -ī,* m.
Wine = *vīnum, -ī,* n.
Wise = *sapiēns, sapientis*
Wish (to), I = *cupiō, -ere, -īvī, -ītum*
With (together with) = *cum* (+ abl.)
Without = *sine* (+ abl.)
Woman = *fēmina, -ae,* f.; *mulier, mulieris,* f.
Word = *verbum, -ī,* n.
Work, I = *labōrō, -āre, -āvī, -ātum*
Worse = *peior, peius*
Worst = *pessimus, -a, -um*
Wound, a = *vulnus, vulneris,* n.
Wound, I = *vulnerō, -āre, -āvī, -ātum*
Wretched = *miser, -era, -erum*
Write, I = *scrībō, -ere, scrīpsī, scrīptum*
Yesterday = *herī*
You (plural) = *vōs*
You (sing.) = *tū*
Young man = *iuvenis, iuvenis,* c.
Your (belonging to you [sing.]) = *tuus, -a, -um*
Your (belonging to you [pl.]) = *vester, vestra,*
    vestrum
Youth, a = *iuvenis, iuvenis,* c.